ROOKIE COACHES WRESTLING GUIDE

American Coaching Effectiveness Program

in cooperation with
USA Wrestling

Leisure Press
Champaign, Illinois

Library of Congress Cataloging-in-Publication Data

Rookie coaches wrestling guide / American Coaching Effectiveness
  Program in cooperation with USA Wrestling.
        p.   cm.
    ISBN 0-88011-421-5
      1. Wrestling--United States--Coaching. I. American Coaching
  Effectiveness Program. II. USA Wrestling.
  GV1196.3.R66 1991   91-20203
  796.8'12--dc20   CIP

ISBN: 0-88011-421-5

Developmental Editor: Ted Miller
Wrestling Consultant: Bob Dellinger/USA Wrestling
Managing Editor and Proofreader: Julia Anderson
Assistant Editors: Elizabeth Bridgett, Jan Seeley
Copyeditor: Carol Hoke
Production Director: Ernie Noa
Typesetters: Kathy Fuoss, Julie Overholt
Text Design: Keith Blomberg
Text Layout: Denise Lowry
Cover Design: Jack Davis
Cover Photo: USA Wrestling
Interior Art: Tim Offenstein, Timothy Stiles
Printer: United Graphics

Leisure Press books are available at special discounts for bulk purchase for sales promotions, premiums, fund-raising, or educational use. Special editions or book excerpts can also be created to specification. For details, contact the Special Sales Manager at Leisure Press.

Printed in the United States of America

10 9 8 7 6 5 4 3 2 1

Leisure Press
A Division of Human Kinetics Publishers, Inc.
Box 5076, Champaign, IL 61825-5076
1-800-747-4457

Canada Office:
Human Kinetics Publishers, Inc.
P.O. Box 2503, Windsor, ON N8Y 4S2
1-800-465-7301 (in Canada only)

UK Office:
Human Kinetics Publishers (UK) Ltd.
P.O. Box 18
Rawdon, Leeds LS19 6TG
England
(0532) 504211

Contents

Welcome to Coaching!

Coaching young athletes is an exciting way to be involved in sport. But it isn't easy. Some coaches are overwhelmed at times by their responsibilities in helping youngsters through early sport experiences. Preparing young people physically and mentally so they can compete effectively, fairly, and safely, and serving as a positive role model are among the difficult but rewarding tasks you accept as a coach.

Whether you are a volunteer club coach or a scholastic coach with a little experience, you already know that youngsters are not mature adults. Young people have different perspectives, experience different emotions, and set different goals than older individuals. They present special challenges to a coach because they react differently than adults to instruction, criticism, encouragement, failure, and success.

This book will help you meet those challenges and experience the rewards of coaching young athletes. It is intended for adults with little or no formal preparation to coach wrestlers.

This *Rookie Coaches Guide* is the result of a joint effort by USA Wrestling and the American Coaching Effectiveness Program (ACEP). The book serves as the Copper Introductory Level text in USA Wrestling's National Coaches Education Program (NCEP). It is the first resource wrestling coaches need to advance to Bronze Leader, Silver Achiever, and Gold Master levels in the NCEP.

USA Wrestling and ACEP hope you will find coaching rewarding and will continue to learn more about coaching and our sport so that you can be the best possible coach for your athletes. Good coaching!

For more information about this coaching education program, please contact

USA Wrestling
National Coaches Education Program
225 South Academy Blvd.
Colorado Springs, CO 80910
(719) 597-8333

UNIT 1

Who, Me . . . a Coach?

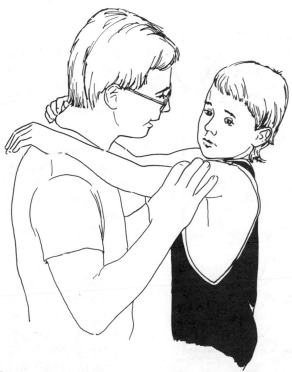

Most club coaches (and many school coaches) are recruited from the ranks of parents, sports fans, and community volunteers. If you are one of these, you probably have not had much formal instruction on how to coach. But when the call went out for help with the wrestling program, you answered because you like kids and enjoy wrestling and because you want to be involved in a worthwhile community activity.

I Want to Help, But . . .

Your first coaching assignment may be difficult. Like many volunteers, you may not know much about the sport you have agreed to coach or about how to work with athletes between the ages of 6 and 16. Relax, because this guide will help you learn the basics of effective coaching. You will find answers to such common questions as these:

- What tools do I need to be a good coach?
- How can I best communicate with my wrestlers?
- What are the basic rules, skills, and strategies of wrestling?
- How do I teach wrestling skills?
- What practice drills will improve my wrestlers' technique?
- What can I do to promote safety?
- What should I do when someone is injured?

Before answering these questions, let's look at what's involved in being a coach.

Am I a Parent or a Coach?

Many coaches are parents, but the two roles should not be confused. As a coach, you are responsible not only to yourself and your child but also to the organization, to all the athletes on the team (including your child), and to their parents. Because of this additional responsibility, your behavior in the wrestling arena will be different from how you act at home, and your child may not understand why.

Imagine the confusion of a kid who is the center of his parent's attention at home but is barely noticed by his parent/coach in the sport setting. You need to explain to your child your new responsibilities and how they will affect your relationship when coaching.

Take the following steps to avoid such problems in coaching your child:

- Ask your child if he wants you to coach the team.
- Explain why you wish to be involved with the team.
- Discuss how your interactions will change when you are coaching at practice or meets.
- Limit your coaching behavior to times when you are acting as coach.

- Avoid acting as a parent during practice or meets to keep your role clear in your child's mind.
- Reaffirm your love for your child without regard to his performance on the mat.

What Are My Responsibilities as a Coach?

A coach must do everything possible to ensure that the youngsters on his team will have an enjoyable and safe experience while they learn sport skills. If you are ever in doubt about your approach, remember the philosophy, *Fun and Fundamentals*.

Provide an Enjoyable Experience

Sports should be fun. Even if nothing else is accomplished, make certain your wrestlers have fun. Take the fun out of sport and you'll take the kids out of sport.

Children enter sport for a number of reasons (e.g., to meet and play with other children, to develop physically, and to learn skills), but their major objective is to have fun. Help them satisfy this goal by injecting humor and variety into your practices. Also, make events nonthreatening, festive experiences for your athletes. Such an approach will increase your wrestlers' desire to participate in the future, which is the primary goal of youth sport. Unit 2 will help you learn how to satisfy your wrestlers' yearning for fun and how to keep winning in perspective. And Unit 3 will describe how you can communicate this perspective to them effectively.

Provide a Safe Experience

You are responsible for planning and teaching activities in such a way that progression between activities minimizes risks (see Units 4 and 5). You must also ensure that the gymnasium in which your team practices and competes is free of hazards. Furthermore, you need to protect yourself from any legal liability that might arise from your involvement as a coach. Unit 5 will help you take appropriate precautions. Finally, wrestlers often adopt unhealthy weight control practices to "make weight." You will be better able to monitor this behavior and advise them on dietary and fitness concerns after you read Unit 7.

Teach Basic Wrestling Skills

In becoming a coach, you take on the role of an educator. You must teach your wrestlers the fundamental skills and strategies necessary for success. That means that you need to "go to school." If you don't know the basics of wrestling now, you can learn them by reading Units 6 and 8 of this manual. But even if you know wrestling as an athlete, do you know how to teach it? This book will help you get started.

Many fine wrestling books are available. And the sport is making great use of videotape to teach coaching philosophy, team organization, and wrestling skills. Both USA Wrestling and ACEP are compiling book and video libraries to help you expand and improve your skills as a wrestling coach. Learning and growing in the sport is fun for the coach as well as the wrestler. So take advantage of these coaching resources.

You'll also find it easier to provide good educational experiences for your wrestlers if you plan your practices. Unit 4 of this manual provides some guidelines.

Getting Help

Veteran coaches in your league are an especially good source of help. They all have experienced the same emotions and conerns you are facing, and their advice can be invaluable as you work through your first season.

You can get more help by watching wrestling coaches at practice and meets, attending clinics, reading wrestling publications, and studying instructional videos. If you are working with beginners, your local high school coach could bring a couple of his wrestlers to one of your practices. Your youngsters would have fun learning from them. If your wrestlers are of high school age themselves, perhaps a nearby college coach would help you out.

Coaching clinics and summer camps are held all across the country, allowing coaches and their young wrestlers to learn beginning, intermediate, and advanced techniques from some of the best teachers in the sport. Such camps and clinics form a major part of USA Wrestling's educational programs.

These two organizations are working hand in hand to provide what you need:

USA Wrestling
225 South Academy Blvd.
Colorado Springs, CO   80910
1-719-597-8333

ACEP
Box 5076
Champaign, IL   61825-5076
1-800-747-4457

Coaching wrestling is a rewarding experience. Your wrestlers will be rewarded if you learn all you can about coaching so you can be the best wrestling coach you can be.

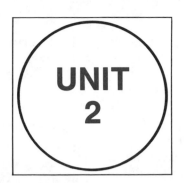

UNIT 2

What Tools Do I Need to Coach?

The traditional coaching tools—things like whistles, coaching clothes, wrestling shoes, and a clipboard—may help you coach, but to be a successful coach, you'll need five other tools that cannot be bought. These tools are available only through self-examination and hard work; they're easy to remember with the acronym COACH:

C—Comprehension

O—Outlook

A—Affection

C—Character

H—Humor

Comprehension

It is essential that you understand the basic rules, skills, and tactics of wrestling. To assist you in *comprehension* of the sport, the second half of this guide describes these elements and suggests how to plan for the season and for individual practices. In Unit 8, you'll find drills to use in developing wrestling skills. To improve your comprehension of wrestling, take the following steps:

• Read Units 6, 7, and 8 of this book.
• Study the wrestling books and instructional videotapes available from USA Wrestling, ACEP, and local stores.
• Contact either USA Wrestling or ACEP, and perhaps a local high school or neighboring collegiate wrestling coach.

- Attend a USA Wrestling Bronze Leader Level clinic—step 2 of the National Coaches Education Program.
- Talk with other, more experienced coaches.
- Watch college, high school, and youth wrestling events in your area.
- Watch wrestling events on television. Videotapes of competitions are available through USA Wrestling.

In addition to having wrestling knowledge, you must use proper training and safety methods so your athletes can participate with little risk of injury. Even then, sport injuries will occur. And more often than not, you'll be the first person responding to your wrestlers' injuries, so be sure you understand the basic emergency procedures described in Unit 5. Also read in that unit how to handle more serious injury situations.

Outlook

This coaching tool refers to your perspective and goals—what you are seeking for your athletes and for yourself as a coach. The most common coaching objectives are: (a) to have fun, (b) to help wrestlers develop their physical, mental, and social skills, and (c) to win. Thus *outlook* involves the priorities you set, your planning, and your vision for the future.

To work successfully with youngsters in sport, you must have your priorities in order. How do you balance the relative merits of fun, development, and victory? You can use the following questions to examine your inner feelings:

Which of these achievements would mean the most to you as a coach?

a. Your wrestlers had a lot of fun and made new friends.

b. Your kids showed marked improvement in their wrestling skills.

c. Your team won the league championship or tournament.

Which statement best reflects your feelings about sport?

a. If it isn't fun for yourself and the kids, it's not worth it.

b. Everyone should learn something new every day.

c. Wrestling can't be fun if you don't win.

How would you like your wrestlers to remember you?

a. As a coach who was really a lot of fun to be around.

b. As a coach who really could teach them how to wrestle.

c. As a coach whose team won a lot of medals and trophies.

What would you most like to hear from one of your wrestlers' parents?

a. Billy really had a good time on the wrestling team this year.

b. Kevin learned some important lessons about wrestling.

c. Mark is so proud of his medals and the team's record.

Which would be the most rewarding moment of your season?

a. Having your team not want to stop, even when practice is over.

b. Seeing one of your wrestlers finally understand about changing levels.

c. Winning the league championship or tournament trophy.

Look over your answers. If most of them are "a" responses, then having fun is most important to you. A majority of "b" answers suggests that skill development is what attracts you to coaching. And if "c" was your most frequent consideration, winning is tops on your list of priorities.

But, in reality, you would probably prefer to answer "all of the above" to each of these questions. It's hard to enjoy anything day after day, week after week, without a feeling of accomplishment, the satisfaction of a job well done, praise for learning a new skill, the satisfaction of scoring a takedown or a reverse, winning a match, getting a fall . . . even *not* being pinned by somebody a lot better. So, fun and fundamentals go hand in hand.

While coaches are quick to agree that fun and development are most important, when they are actually coaching, some place far

too much emphasis on winning. You will face situations that challenge *you* to keep winning in its proper perspective. At such moments you'll have to choose between your wrestlers' development and winning. If your priorities are in order, your kids' well-being will take precedence over win-loss records every time. Take the following actions to better define your outlook:

- Determine your priorities for the season before you start.
- Prepare for situations that challenge your priorities.
- Set goals for yourself and your wrestlers that are reasonable and consistent with those priorities. Your objectives should not be an impossible dream.
- Plan how you and your wrestlers can best attain those goals.
- Review your goals frequently to be sure that you are staying on track.

It is particularly important for coaches to give all young athletes an opportunity to take part. Each youngster should have an opportunity to have fun, to develop his skills, and to test them in competition. This may mean that you do not always put your best team on the mat, and it may mean that you have to seek out novice and "B team" events to give some kids a better chance for success. It definitely means that you will not spend all of your time coaching only the best athletes.

Remember that the challenge and joy of sport is experienced through *striving* to win, not through winning itself. Wrestlers who aren't allowed to suit up are denied the opportunity to strive for victory. And herein lies the irony—a coach who encourages all his wrestlers to participate and develop their skills will, in the end, come out on top.

Athletes First, Winning Second

ACEP's motto will help you keep your outlook in the best interest of the kids in your wrestling room. It summarizes in four words all you need to remember when you establish your coaching priorities. This motto recognizes that striving to win is an important, even vital, part of sport. But it emphatically states that no efforts in striving to win should be made at the expense of athletes' well-being, development, and enjoyment.

Affection

This is another vital tool you'll need in your coaching kit . . . a genuine concern for the young people you coach. It involves having a love for kids, a desire to share with them your love and knowledge of the sport, and the patience and understanding that allows

each individual wrestler to grow from his involvement in sport.

Successful coaches have a real concern for the health and welfare of their wrestlers. They care that each kid on the team has an enjoyable and successful experience. They have a strong desire to work with kids and be involved in their growth. And they have the patience to work with those who are slower to learn or less capable of performing. If you have such qualities or are willing to work hard to develop them, then you have the *affection* necessary to coach young athletes.

There are many ways to demonstrate your affection and patience, including these:

- Make an effort to get to know each wrestler on your team. Call them by name.
- Treat each young athlete as an individual.
- Empathize with kids trying to learn new and difficult wrestling techniques.
- Treat your athletes as you would like to be treated under similar circumstances.
- Stay in control of your emotions.
- Show your enthusiasm for being involved with your team.
- Keep an upbeat and positive tone in all of your communications.

Character

Youngsters learn by listening to what adults say. But they learn even more by watching the behavior of certain important individuals. As a coach, you are likely to be a significant figure in the lives of your athletes. Will you be a good role model?

Having good *character* means modeling appropriate behaviors for sport and life. That means more than just saying the right things. What you say and what you do must match. There is no place for the "Do as I say, not as I do" philosophy. Be in control before, during, and after all practices and meets. And don't be afraid to admit that you were wrong. No one is perfect!

Consider the following steps to being a good role model:

- Take stock of your strengths and weaknesses.
- Build on your strengths.
- Set goals for yourself to improve those areas you would not like to see imitated.
- If you slip up, apologize to your team and to yourself. You'll do better next time.

Humor

Often overlooked as a coaching tool, *humor* means having the ability to laugh *at* yourself and *with* your athletes during practices and meets. Nothing helps balance the tone of a serious, skill-learning session like a chuckle or two. And a sense of humor puts in perspective the many mistakes your young wrestlers will make. So don't get upset over each miscue or respond negatively to erring wrestlers. Allow them and yourself to enjoy the "ups" and don't dwell on the "downs."

Here are some tips for injecting humor into your practices:

- Make practices fun by including a variety of activities.
- Keep all wrestlers involved in drills and workouts.
- Consider laughter by your wrestlers a sign of enjoyment, not a lack of discipline.
- Smile!

Where Do You Stand?

To take stock of your "coaching tool kit," rank yourself on three questions for each of the five coaching tools. Circle the number that best describes your *present* status on each item.

Not at all		Somewhat		Very much so
1	2	3	4	5

Comprehension

1. Could you explain the rules of wrestling without a lot of study?   1   2   3   4   5
2. Do you know how to organize and conduct safe wrestling practices?   1   2   3   4   5
3. Do you know how to provide first aid for common minor injuries?   1   2   3   4   5

Comprehension Score: _____

Outlook

4. Do you have winning in its proper perspective when you coach?   1   2   3   4   5
5. Do you prepare a plan for every meeting and practice?   1   2   3   4   5
6. Do you have a vision of what you want your wrestlers to be able to do by the end of the season?   1   2   3   4   5

Outlook Score: _____

Affection

7. Do you enjoy working with kids?   1   2   3   4   5
8. Are you patient with youngsters learning new techniques?   1   2   3   4   5
9. Are you able to show your wrestlers that you care?   1   2   3   4   5

Affection Score: _____

Character

10. Are your words and behavior consistent with each other?   1   2   3   4   5
11. Are you a good model for your wrestlers?   1   2   3   4   5
12. Do you keep negative emotions under control before, during, and after competition?   1   2   3   4   5

Character Score: _____

Humor

13. Do you usually smile at your wrestlers?   1   2   3   4   5
14. Are your practices fun learning experiences for your wrestlers?   1   2   3   4   5
15. Are you able to laugh at your mistakes?   1   2   3   4   5

Humor Score: _____

If you scored 9 or less on any of the coaching tools, be sure to reread those sections carefully. And even if you scored 15 on each tool, don't be complacent. Keep learning! Then you'll be well-equipped with the tools you need to coach young athletes.

UNIT 3

How Should I Communicate With My Wrestlers?

ow you know the tools needed to COACH: Comprehension, Outlook, Affection, Character, and Humor. These are essentials for effective coaching; without them, you'd have a difficult time getting started. But none of those tools will work if you don't know how to use them with your athletes—and this requires skillful communication. This unit examines what communication is and how you can become a more effective communicator-coach.

What's Involved in Communication?

Coaches often mistakenly believe that communication involves only instructing wrestlers to do something, but verbal commands are only a small part of the communication process. More than half of what is communicated is nonverbal. So remember when you are coaching, "Actions speak louder than words."

Communication in its simplest form involves two people: a *sender* and a *receiver*.

The sender transmits the message verbally, through facial expression, and/or through body language. Once the message is sent, it depends on the receiver whether the message is transmitted successfully. A receiver who fails to listen or pay attention will miss part, if not all, of the message. Often you can tell whether the message is getting through by looking at the expression on the receiver's face.

How Can I Send More Effective Messages?

Young athletes often have little understanding of the rules and skills of wrestling and probably even less confidence about performing in competition. So they need accurate, understandable, and supportive messages to help them along. That's why your verbal and nonverbal messages are so important.

Verbal Messages

"Sticks and stones may break my bones, but words will never hurt me" isn't true. Spoken words can and do have a strong and long-lasting effect. And coaches' words are particularly influential because youngsters place great importance on what coaches say. Perhaps you, like many former youth sport participants, have a difficult time recalling

anything you were told by your elementary teacher but can still recall several specific things said to you by your coaches at that time. Such is the lasting effect of a coach's comments to his athletes.

Whether you are correcting misbehavior, teaching a wrestler how to execute a fireman's carry, or praising a wrestler for good effort, you should consider several things when sending a message verbally. They include the following:

- *Be positive, but honest.*
- *State it clearly and simply.*
- *Say it loud enough, and say it again.*
- *Send consistent messages.*

Be Positive, but Honest

Nothing turns people off like hearing someone nag all the time, and young athletes react the same way to a coach who gripes constantly. Kids particularly need encouragement because they often doubt their ability to perform in sport. So *look* for and *tell* your wrestlers what they did well.

But don't cover up poor or incorrect technique with rosy words of praise. Kids know all too well when they've made a mistake, and no cheerful cliché can undo their errors. If you fail to acknowledge wrestlers' mistakes, your athletes will think you are a phony.

Compliment Sandwich

A good way to handle situations in which you have identified and must correct improper technique is to serve your wrestlers a ''compliment'' sandwich:

1. Point out what the athlete did correctly.
2. Let the wrestler know what was incorrect, and instruct him how to correct it.
3. Encourage the wrestler by reemphasizing what he did well.

State It Clearly and Simply

Positive and honest messages are good, but only if expressed directly and in words your wrestlers understand. "Beating around the bush" is ineffective. And if you ramble, your wrestlers will miss the point of your message and probably will lose interest. Here are some tips for saying things clearly.

- Organize your thoughts before speaking to your athletes.
- Explain things thoroughly, but don't bore them with long-winded monologues.
- Use language your wrestlers can understand, but avoid trying to be "hip" by using their age group's slang.

Say It Loud Enough, and Say It Again

Talk to your team in a voice that all members can hear and interpret. A crisp, vigorous voice commands attention and respect; garbled and weak speech is tuned out. It's appropriate to soften your voice when speaking to an individual wrestler about a personal problem. But most of the time your messages will be for all your wrestlers to hear, so make sure they can! An enthusiastic voice also motivates wrestlers and tells them you enjoy being their coach.

Sometimes what you say, even if stated loud and clearly, won't sink in the first time.

This may be particularly true with young athletes hearing words they don't understand. To help get new ideas across, explain them as part of a concept or framework. It's very important to use consistent terminology in teaching. Once you get an idea across, stick with the same words as reminders. If you want a wrestler to lower his level by getting his hips down, keep reminding him "Hips down, hips down!" Don't confuse him with "Lower your level," even though in this case it means the same thing.

Send Consistent Messages

People often say things in ways that imply a different message. For example, a touch of sarcasm in the words "way to go" sends an entirely different message than the words themselves. Avoid sending mixed messages. Keep the tone of your voice consistent with the words you use. And don't say something one day and contradict it the next; your wrestlers will get their wires crossed.

Nonverbal Messages

Keep your verbal and nonverbal messages consistent. Don't shake your head, indicating disapproval, while telling a wrestler "nice try." Which is the wrestler to believe, your gesture or your words?

Messages can be sent nonverbally in a number of ways. Facial expressions and body language are just two of the more obvious forms of nonverbal signals that can help you communicate with your wrestlers when you coach.

Facial Expressions

The look on a person's face is the quickest clue to what he thinks or feels. Your wrestlers know this, so they will study your face, looking for any sign that will tell them more than the words you say. Don't try to fool them by putting on a happy or blank "mask." They'll see through it, and you'll lose credibility.

Serious, stone-faced expressions are no help to kids who need cues as to how they are performing. They will just assume you're unhappy or disinterested. Don't be afraid to smile. A smile from a coach can give a great boost to an unsure young athlete. Plus, a smile lets your wrestlers know that you are happy coaching them. But don't overdo it, or your wrestlers won't be able to tell when you are genuinely pleased by something they've done or when you are just "putting on" a smiling face.

Body Language

How would your wrestlers think you felt if you came to practice slouched over, with head down and shoulders slumped? Tired? Bored? Unhappy? How would they think you felt if you watched them during a match with your hands on your hips, your jaw clenched, and your face reddened? Upset with them? Disgusted at the official? Mad at a fan? Probably some or all of these things would enter your wrestlers' minds. And none of these impressions is the kind you want your wrestlers to have of you. That's why you should carry yourself in a pleasant, confident, and vigorous manner. Such a posture not only projects happiness with your coaching role but also provides a good example for your young wrestlers who may model your behavior.

Physical contact also can be a very important use of body language. Obviously, you will have a lot of physical contact with your wrestlers during instruction and demonstrations. But a handshake, a pat on the head, an arm around the shoulder, or even a big bear hug are effective ways of showing approval, concern, affection, and joy to your wrestlers. Youngsters are especially in need of these types of nonverbal messages.

How Can I Improve My Receiving Skills?

Now let's examine the other half of the communication process—receiving messages. Too many people are very good senders and very poor receivers. As a coach of young athletes, it is essential that you both send and receive effectively.

Receiving skills are simple, but perhaps less satisfying than sending skills. People naturally enjoy hearing themselves talk more than others. But if you are willing to learn the keys to receiving messages and make a strong effort to use them with your wrestlers, you'll be surprised to discover what you've been missing.

Attention!

First you must pay attention; you must want to hear what others have to communicate to you. That's not always easy when you're busy coaching and have many things competing for your attention. But in one-to-one or team meetings with wrestlers, you must *focus on what they are telling you*, both verbally and nonverbally. You'll be amazed at the little signals you pick up. Not only will such focused attention help you catch every word your wrestlers say, but you'll notice your wrestlers' moods and physical states, and you'll get an idea of your wrestlers' feelings toward you and other members of the team.

Listen CARE-FULLY

How we receive messages from others, perhaps more than anything else we do, demonstrates how much we care for the sender and what that person has to tell us. If you care little for your wrestlers or have little regard for what they have to say, it will show in how you attend and listen to them. Check yourself. Do you find your mind wandering to what you are going to do after practice while one of your wrestlers is talking to you? Do you frequently have to ask your wrestlers, "What did you say?" If so, you need to work on your receiving mechanics of attending and listening. But perhaps the

most critical question you should ask yourself, if you find that you're missing the messages your wrestlers send, is this: Do I care?

How Do I Put It All Together?

So far we've discussed separately the sending and receiving of messages. But we all know that senders and receivers switch roles several times during an interaction. One person initiates a communication by sending a message to another person who receives the message. The receiver then switches roles and becomes the sender by responding to the person who sent the initial message. These verbal and nonverbal responses are called *feedback*.

Your wrestlers will be looking to you for feedback all the time. They will want to know how you think they are performing, what you think of their ideas, and whether

their efforts please you. Obviously, you can respond in many different ways. *How you respond* will strongly affect your wrestlers. So let's take a look at a few general types of feedback and examine their possible effects.

Providing Instructions

With young wrestlers, much of your feedback will involve answering questions about how to perform certain techniques. Your instructive responses to these questions should include both verbal and nonverbal feedback. Here are some suggestions for giving instructional feedback:

- Use demonstrations to provide nonverbal instructional feedback (see Unit 4).
- Keep verbal instructions simple and concise.
- Use the "whole-part-whole" teaching method. Demonstrate the whole maneuver. Then show the various parts—setup, execution, follow-through—explaining how the basic skills of stance, motion, penetration, and so on, affect the technique. Then put all the parts together again to make the whole maneuver.
- "Walk" wrestlers through the technique at a moderate pace and against passive resistance until they learn the proper steps. Then have them work at increased speeds and against increased resistance.

Correcting Errors

When your wrestlers execute incorrectly, you need to provide informative feedback to correct the error—the sooner the better. When you do correct mistakes, keep in mind these two principles: Use negative criticism sparingly, and keep calm.

Use Negative Criticism Sparingly

Although you may need to punish athletes for horseplay or dangerous activities by scolding or removing them from activities temporarily, don't reprimand wrestlers for performance errors. Admonishing wrestlers for honest mistakes makes them afraid to even try.

Nothing ruins a youngster's enjoyment of a sport more than a coach who harps on every miscue. So correct your athletes with a positive approach. Your wrestlers will enjoy wrestling more, and you'll enjoy coaching more. Try complimenting those actions that are correct, while encouraging the youngster to repeat and correct the actions performed improperly.

Keep Calm

Don't fly off the handle when your wrestlers make mistakes. Remember, you're coaching young and inexperienced athletes, not highly skilled adults. You'll see more incorrect than correct techniques, and you'll probably have more discipline problems than you expect. But throwing a tantrum over each error or misbehavior will only inhibit your wrestlers or suggest to them the wrong kind of behavior to model. So let your wrestlers know that mistakes aren't the end of the world; stay cool!

Giving Positive Feedback

Praising wrestlers when they have performed or behaved well is an effective way of getting them to repeat or try to repeat that performance in the future. And positive feedback for effort is an especially effective way

Coaches, be positive!

Only a very small percentage of ACEP-trained coaches' behaviors are negative.

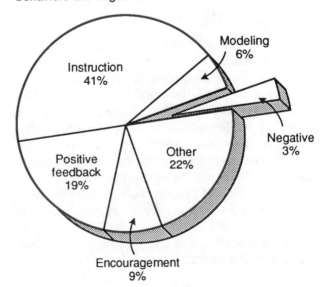

to motivate youngsters to work on difficult skills. So, rather than shouting and providing negative feedback to a wrestler who has made a mistake, offer him a compliment sandwich.

Merely the way you word feedback can make it more positive than negative. For example, instead of saying, "Don't just stand there!" you might say, "Motion . . . move your feet . . . move your opponent!" Then your wrestlers will be focusing on *what to do* instead of what *not* to do.

You can give positive feedback verbally and nonverbally. Telling a wrestler, especially in front of teammates, that he has executed well is a great way to boost the confidence of a youngster. And a pat on the back or a handshake can be a very tangible way of communicating your recognition of a wrestler's performance.

Whom Else Do I Need to Communicate With?

Coaching involves not only sending and receiving messages and providing feedback to wrestlers but also interacting with parents, fans, officials, and opposing coaches. If you don't communicate effectively with these people, your coaching career will be short-lived. So try the following suggestions for communicating with these groups.

Parents

A wrestler's parents need to be assured that their child is under the direction of a coach who knows the sport and is concerned about their youngster's well-being. You should hold a preseason meeting in which you describe your background and your approach to coaching. Holding such a meeting in conjunction with a potluck dinner is a good way to get to know wrestlers' moms and dads. Let them know what you expect of them and how they can help the program.

If parents contact you with a concern during the season, listen closely and try to offer positive responses. If you need to communicate with parents, catch them after a practice, give them a phone call, or send a note through the mail. Messages sent to parents through kids are too often lost, misinterpreted, or forgotten.

Fans

The stands probably won't be overflowing at your meets, but that only means that you'll more easily hear the few fans who criticize your coaching. When you hear something negative said about the job you're doing, don't respond. Keep calm, consider whether the message had any value, and, if not, forget it. Acknowledging critical, unwarranted comments from a fan during a match will only encourage others to voice their opinions. So put away your "rabbit ears" and communicate to fans through your actions that you are a confident, competent coach.

Officials

How you communicate with officials will have a great influence on the way your wrestlers behave toward them. You must set a good example. Greet officials with a handshake, an introduction, and perhaps some casual conversation about the upcoming meet. Indicate your respect for them before, during, and after the match. Don't make critical remarks, shout, or use disrespectful gestures. Your wrestlers will see you do it, and they'll get the idea that such behavior is appropriate.

And, if the official hears or sees you, the communication between the two of you will break down. Don't try to referee from your coach's chair. He's the official, you're the coach. Neither you nor your wrestlers should try to influence the referee's calls. There's a good chance that you'll influence his calls *against* your wrestler. Or your wrestler can become so concerned about the officiating that he loses his focus on his strategy and his opponent.

Opposing Coaches

Make an effort to visit with the coach of the opposing team before the meet. Perhaps the two of you can work out a special arrangement for the competition, maybe pairing up some spare wrestlers in additional matches.

During the competition, don't get into a personal feud with the opposing coaches. Remember, it's the kids, not the coaches, who are competing. And by getting along well with the opposing coach, you'll show your wrestlers that competition involves sportsmanship.

Summary Checklist

Check your communication skills by answering "Yes" or "No" to the following:

	Yes	No
1. Are your verbal messages to your wrestlers positive and honest?	——	——
2. Do you speak loudly, clearly, and in words your athletes can understand?	——	——
3. Do you remember to repeat instructions to your wrestlers in case they didn't hear you the first time?	——	——
4. Are the tone of your voice and your nonverbal messages consistent with the words you use?	——	——
5. Do your facial expressions and body language express interest in and happiness with your coaching role?	——	——
6. Are you attentive to your wrestlers and able to pick up even their small verbal and nonverbal messages?	——	——
7. Do you really care about what your athletes say to you?	——	——
8. Do you instruct rather than criticize when your wrestlers make mistakes?	——	——
9. Are you usually positive when responding to things your athletes say and do?	——	——
10. Do you try to communicate in a cooperative and respectful manner with wrestlers' parents, the fans, officials, and opposing coaches?	——	——

If you answered "No" to any of these questions, you may want to go back to the section of this chapter where the topic was discussed. *Now* is the time to address communication problems, not when you're coaching your athletes.

UNIT 4

How Do I Get My Wrestlers Ready to Compete?

To coach wrestling, you must understand the basic elements of the sport. The second part of this guide provides information on rules, skills, and tactics that you need to comprehend wrestling.

But all the wrestling knowledge in the world will do you little good unless you can present it effectively to your wrestlers. That's why this unit is so important. Here you will learn ways to teach sport skills and guidelines for planning your season and practices.

How Do I Teach Sport Skills?

Many people believe that the only qualification needed to coach is to have competed in the sport. It's helpful to have wrestled, but there is much more to coaching successfully. Some of the sport's greatest coaches—Hall of Famers Ed Gallagher, Paul Keen, Charles Mayser, Dave McCuskey, Sprig Gardner, and Walter O'Connell, for example—never wrestled at all. So, even if you haven't wrestled, you can learn to coach with this IDEA:

I —Introduce the skill.

D—Demonstrate the skill.

E—Explain the skill.

A—Attend to wrestlers practicing the skill.

Introduce the Skill

Young and inexperienced wrestlers need to know what skill they are learning and why they are learning it. Therefore, you should take these three steps every time you introduce a skill to your athletes:

1. Get your wrestlers' attention.
2. Name the skill or technique.
3. Explain the importance of the skill.

Get Your Wrestlers' Attention

Because youngsters are easily distracted, use some method to get their attention. Some coaches use interesting news items or old wrestling stories. Others use jokes. And others simply project an enthusiasm that gets their kids to listen. Whatever method you use, speak slightly above normal volume and look your wrestlers in the eye when you speak.

Whenever possible, stand with your back toward a wall so the wrestlers won't be distracted. Arrange the wrestlers in a semicircle one or two rows deep. Then you won't have to keep turning around as you speak and demonstrate. Ask if all can see and hear you before you begin.

Name the Skill or Technique

Each of the Seven Basic Skills has a name. Use them. Specific maneuvers and techniques sometimes have more than one name. Decide which name you'll use and stick with it to avoid confusion and help your wrestlers understand.

Explain the Importance of the Skill

Although you may know the importance of a skill, your kids may not be able to realize immediately how it will help them become better wrestlers. Because almost all wrestling maneuvers are based upon one or more of the Seven Basic Skills, it's important that they understand the relationship between a Basic Skill (e.g., motion, penetration, changing levels) and a type of maneuver (e.g., single leg, duck-under, high crotch). Your explanation of the skill should help them make the connection.

The most difficult aspect of coaching is this: Coaches must learn to let athletes learn. Sport skills should be taught so they have meaning to the child, not just meaning to the coach.

Rainer Martens, ACEP Founder

Demonstrate the Skill

The demonstration step is the most important part of teaching sport skills to young wrestlers who may never have done anything closely resembling the maneuver.

They need a picture, not just words. They need to *see* how the skill is performed.

If you are unable to perform the skill correctly, have an assistant coach or someone more experienced on the mat perform the demonstration. These tips will help make your demonstrations more effective:

- Use correct form.
- Demonstrate the skill or maneuver several times.
- Slow down the action during one or two performances so the wrestlers can see every movement involved.
- Perform the maneuver at different angles so your wrestlers can get it in full perspective.
- Demonstrate the technique to both the right and left sides.

Explain the Skill

Wrestlers learn more effectively when they're given a brief explanation of the maneuver and the basic skill behind it along with the demonstration. Use simple terms and, if possible, relate the technique to skills they've already learned. Ask your wrestlers whether they understand your description. If someone looks confused, have him explain the skill back to you. At the next practice, ask one or more of your wrestlers to demonstrate this skill for the group.

Complex techniques often are better understood when they are explained in manageable parts. For instance, if you want to teach your wrestlers how to set up, execute, and follow through on a duck-under, you might take the following steps:

1. Explain the technique and demonstrate the complete action.
2. Break down the maneuver and point out its component parts to your wrestlers.
   - Show beginning position and motion, and explain why the maneuver must be built on this foundation.
   - Show how changing levels and penetration are vital to the execution.
   - Demonstrate how to finish the move and score with it.
3. Have the wrestlers concentrate on each of the individual skills that make up this technique, such as motion, changing levels, penetration, and lift.
4. After the wrestlers have demonstrated their ability to perform the separate parts of the technique in sequence, have them go through the entire maneuver from start to finish.
5. Again explain the entire maneuver and have the wrestlers practice it on each other with the defensive wrestler at first offering only "passive" resistance.

Attend to Wrestlers Practicing the Skill

If the technique you selected was within your wrestlers' capabilities and you have done an effective job of introducing, demonstrating, and explaining it, your wrestlers should be ready to attempt the skill. Some wrestlers may need to be physically guided through the movements during their first few attempts. Guiding unsure athletes through the maneuver in this way will help them gain confidence to perform it on their own.

Your teaching duties don't end when all your athletes have demonstrated that they understand how to perform the technique. In fact, a significant part of your teaching will involve observing closely the hit-and-miss trial performances of your wrestlers.

As you observe their errors in drills and activities, offer positive, corrective feedback in the form of the "compliment sandwich" described in Unit 3. If a wrestler performs the skill properly, acknowledge it with enthusiasm and offer praise. Keep in mind that your feedback will have a great influence on your athletes' motivation to practice and improve their performance.

In the teaching of any wrestling maneuver, it is only natural for the wrestler defending himself against a technique to want to resist and to "fight back." Remind the defensive member of each pair to offer only token

resistance at first, to "go with the flow" of the technique until his workout partner feels that he has learned to assemble the components of the move. Then defensive resistance can be gradually increased during the learning process.

Reaction to the technique and counterattack can be part of the next lesson. Don't get into the use of counterattacks immediately. Typically, counters are learned quickly and only serve to prevent the other wrestler from learning the offensive technique well enough to try it with any success.

Remember that young athletes need individual instruction. So move around the room and watch each wrestler in turn. Be prepared to give individual help during and after practice or before the next practice begins.

Wrestlers respond well to coaches who show their concern with action and enthusiasm. They like a coach who moves around the room and demonstrates to them that it's important to him that they learn. Then it becomes more important to the kids.

What Planning Do I Need to Do?

Some coaches make the mistake of showing up for the first practice with no particular plan in mind. These coaches find that their practices are unorganized, their wrestlers are frustrated and inattentive, and the amount and quality of their instruction is limited. Planning is essential to successful teaching *and* coaching. And it doesn't begin on the way to practice!

Preseason Planning

Effective coaches begin planning well before the start of the season. Here are some preseason steps that will make the season more enjoyable, successful, and safe for you and your wrestlers:

- Familiarize yourself with the sport organization in which you are involved, especially its philosophy and goals regarding youth sport.
- Examine the availability of facilities, equipment, instructional aids, and other materials needed for practices and competition.
- Be sure your club membership is up to date, and you have liability insurance to cover you if one of your athletes is hurt (see Unit 5).
- Establish your coaching priorities regarding fun, developing wrestlers' skills, and winning.
- Meet with your assistant coaches to discuss the philosophy, goals, team rules, and plans for the season.
- Register wrestlers for the team. Have each one complete an athlete informa-

tion form and undergo a medical examination.

- Develop a conditioning, nutrition, and injury prevention program for your wrestlers.
- Hold a parent orientation meeting to inform parents of your background, philosophy, goals, and instructional approach. Also give a brief overview of wrestling rules, terms, and techniques to familiarize parents with the sport.
- Enlist volunteers to help during the season—driving wrestlers to and from meets, taking tickets, operating concession stands, keeping track of registration and entry fees, and so on.

You may be surprised at the number of things you should do even before the first practice. But if you address them during the preseason, the season will be much more enjoyable and productive for you and for your wrestlers.

In-Season Planning

Your activities during the season should be based on whether they will help your wrestlers develop physical and mental skills, learn rules, tactics, sportsmanship, and grow to love the sport. All of these goals are important, but we'll focus on the skills and techniques of wrestling to give you an idea of how to itemize your objectives.

Goal Setting

What you plan to do during the season must be reasonable for the maturity and skill level of your wrestlers. Because almost every technique, maneuver, and tactic in wrestling is based upon the Seven Basic Skills, you have to be sure your wrestlers thoroughly understand these skills before moving on to specific techniques. If you have very young, beginning wrestlers, teaching the Seven Basic Skills may be just about all you accomplish during the season. Even if your kids have wrestling experience, you should review the Seven Basic Skills on a regular basis.

To begin the season, your instructional goals might include the following:

- Wrestlers will run, perform calisthenics, and stretch their muscles to prepare properly for exertion.
- Wrestlers will review the first Basic Skill of *position*, demonstrating the proper relationship of the head, back, hips, feet, hands, elbows, knees, and chest.
- Wrestlers will learn the importance of *motion*, the ability to move freely and to keep the opponent moving.
- Wrestlers will understand the necessity for *changing levels* to properly execute a wide variety of techniques.
- Wrestlers will be able to demonstrate *penetration* of the opponent's position, thereby reducing his stability.
- Wrestlers will be able to integrate *lifting* into the execution of scoring techniques.
- Wrestlers will be able to execute the *back step* as the basis of a variety of maneuvers.
- Wrestlers will demonstrate knowledge of the *back arch* as a requirement for throws as well as for a variety of low-level scoring attacks.

Wrestling is the most natural activity in sport. Even a mere toddler will grab a playmate, try to knock him off his feet, then try to get on top of him. A wrestling coach's job is to channel a child's natural play activity into sport and to teach him proper techniques and sportsmanship.

Organizing

After you've defined the skills, techniques, and tactics you want your wrestlers to learn during the season, you can plan how to teach them to your wrestlers in practice. But be flexible! If your wrestlers are having difficulty learning a skill or technique, take some extra time until they get the hang of it—even if that means moving back your schedule. After all, if your wrestlers are unable to perform the fundamental skills, they'll never execute the more complex skills you have scheduled for them.

Still, it helps to have a plan for advancing wrestlers through skills and maneuvers during the season. The 8-week sample season plan in the appendix shows how to schedule your skill instruction in an organized and progressive manner. If this is your first coaching experience, you may wish to follow the plan as it stands. If you have some previous experience, you may want to modify the schedule to better fit the needs of your team.

What Makes Up a Good Practice?

A good instructional plan makes practice preparation much easier. In early season practice, have wrestlers work on the Seven Basic Skills, then introduce those techniques that take the longest to learn and those that are prerequisite to other maneuvers.

It helps to establish *one objective* for each practice, but try to include a *variety of activities* related to that objective. For example, although your primary objective might be to enhance the wrestlers' gut wrench technique, you should have wrestlers perform several different drills designed to strengthen their bridge position. To add more variety to your practices, vary the order of activities.

In general, we recommend that each of your practices includes the following:

- *Warm up*
- *Review and practice previously taught skills*
- *Teach and practice new techniques*
- *Drill in competitive conditions or scrimmages*
- *Cool down*
- *Evaluate*

Warm Up

As you're checking the roster and announcing practice objectives, your wrestlers should be preparing their bodies for vigorous activity. A 5- to 15-minute period of easy-paced activities, stretching, and calisthenics should be enough for youngsters to limber their muscles and reduce the risk of injury.

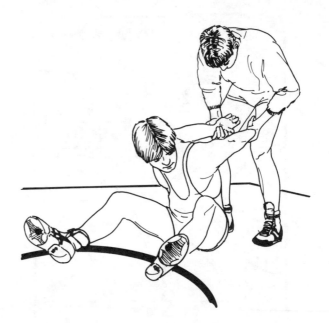

Review and Practice Previously Taught Skills

Devote part of each practice to having wrestlers work on the fundamentals they have already learned. But remember, kids like variety. Organize and modify drills so that everyone is involved and stays interested.

Praise and encourage kids when you notice improvement, and offer individual assistance to those who need help.

Teach and Practice New Techniques

Gradually build on your wrestlers' existing techniques by giving them something new to practice each session. Refer to Unit 8 for a description of the skills you will want wrestlers to learn and develop.

Drill in Competitive Conditions or Scrimmages

Competition among teammates during practice prepares wrestlers for actual matches and informs young athletes about their abilities relative to those of their peers. Youngsters also seem to have more fun in competitive activities.

You can create matchlike conditions by using competitive drills with short bursts of action and modified match conditions (see Units 6 and 8). However, consider the following guidelines before introducing competition into your practices.

- Provide all wrestlers an equal opportunity to participate.
- Match the wrestlers by size, maturity, and ability.
- Require the wrestlers to execute fundamentals before they are allowed to compete.
- Emphasize improvement and performing to capability, rather than winning.
- Give wrestlers room to make mistakes by avoiding constant evaluation and comments.

Cool Down

Each practice should wind down with a 5- to 10-minute period of light exercise, including jogging, performance of simple skills, and some stretching. The cool-down allows athletes' bodies to return to the resting state and avoid stiffness, and it affords you an opportunity to review the practice.

Evaluate

At the end of practice spend a few minutes with your wrestlers reviewing how well the session accomplished the objective you had set. Even if your evaluation is negative, express "positive criticism," show optimism for future practices, and send wrestlers off on an upbeat note.

How Do I Put a Practice Together?

Simply knowing the components of practice is not enough. You also must be able to arrange those components into a logical progression and fit them into a time schedule. Now, using your instructional goals as a guide for selecting what skills to have your wrestlers work on, try to plan several wrestling practices you might conduct. The following example should help you get started.

Sample Practice Plan

Performance Objective. Wrestlers will learn to execute a duck-under for a takedown.

Component	Time*	Activity or drill
Warm up	10 minutes	Jog and skip around the mat. Stretching exercises.
Review	15 minutes	Position, motion, changing levels, penetration, lifting, and drills on previously learned techniques.
Teach	10 minutes	Setup, execution, and follow-through of the duck-under.
Practice	15 minutes	Work on tie-ups and duck-under execution to either side with partner applying passive resistance.
Drill	10 minutes	Thirty-second bursts against increasing resistance.
Scrimmage	10 minutes	One-minute periods, wrestlers starting even and on their feet, trying duck-unders and other types of takedowns.
Conditioning	10 minutes	Varied competition and strenuous exercises.
Cool down and evaluate	10 minutes	Easy jogging and stretching; individual question-and-answer period.

*Be flexible. If any component takes longer than the time you have allowed, reduce later elements of the schedule so the total practice time remains consistent. Do not lengthen the practice. Discipline yourself to finish in the time allotted . . . it will make you a better coach.

Summary Checklist

During your wrestling season, check your teaching and planning skills periodically. As you gain more coaching experience, you should be able to answer "Yes" to each of the following.

When you teach skills and techniques to your wrestlers, do you

____ arrange the wrestlers so all can see and hear, with your back to the wall?

____ introduce the technique clearly and relate it to the Seven Basic Skills?

____ demonstrate the technique properly several times?

____ explain the technique simply and accurately?

____ closely attend the wrestlers practicing the technique?

____ offer corrective, positive feedback or praise after watching wrestlers try the maneuver?

When you plan, do you remember to plan for

_____ preseason events such as registration of wrestlers, medical examinations, insurance protection, use of facilities, and parent orientation?

_____ a volunteer support group to assist with dual meets, tournaments, and travel?

_____ season goals such as the development of wrestlers' physical skills, mental skills, sportsmanship, and enjoyment?

_____ practice components such as warm-up, review of previously taught skills, teaching and practicing new techniques, practicing under competitive conditions, cool-down, and evaluation?

UNIT 5

What Can I Do for Safety?

One of your wrestlers is struggling to keep from getting pinned. To your relief, time runs out and the period is over. The opponent stands up and walks to the side of the mat. But you see that your wrestler is still lying on the mat and appears to be in pain. What do you do?

 One of the least pleasant aspects of coaching is seeing wrestlers get hurt. Fortunately, there are many steps coaches can take to reduce the risk of injury. But in spite of such efforts, injury remains a reality of sport, particularly a "combat" sport such as wrestling. So you must be prepared to give first aid when injuries occur and to protect yourself against unjustified lawsuits. This unit will describe how you can

- create the safest possible environment for your wrestlers,

- provide emergency first aid to wrestlers when they get hurt, and
- protect yourself from injury liability.

How Do I Keep My Wrestlers From Getting Hurt?

Injuries may occur because of poor preventive measures. Part of your planning, described in Unit 4, should include steps that give your wrestlers the best possible chance for injury-free participation. These steps include the following:

- Preseason physical examination
- Physical conditioning
- Inspection of facilities and equipment
- Matching athletes by size, physical maturity and experience, and warning of inherent risks
- Demonstration of illegal and potentially dangerous holds and situations
- Proper supervision and record keeping
- Mandatory warm-up and cool-down

Preseason Physical Examination

Even in the absence of severe injury, ongoing illness, or medical handicap (such as diabetes), your wrestlers should have a physical examination every year before the start of practice. If a wrestler has a known complication, a physician's consent should be obtained before participation is allowed. Once a wrestler has been sidelined for any length of time by an injury, a physician's ex-amination and consent should be obtained before the wrestler returns to the mat.

You should also have the wrestlers' parents or guardians sign participation agreement forms and release forms that allow their children to be treated in case of emergency. Keep copies of these release forms in your first aid kit so you have them on hand at each practice or competition.

Physical Conditioning

Muscles, tendons, and ligaments unaccustomed to vigorous and long-lasting physical activity are prone to injury. Therefore, prepare your athletes to withstand the exertion of competing in your sport. An effective conditioning program for wrestling involves running and other forms of aerobic and anaerobic activity.

Make conditioning drills and activities fun. Include a skill component, such as bridging, or arrange competitions to prevent wrestlers from becoming bored or looking upon the activity as "work."

INFORMED CONSENT FORM

I hereby give my permission for _____ to participate in

_____ during the athletic season beginning in 199___. Further, I authorize the school to provide emergency treatment of an injury to or illness of my child if qualified medical personnel consider treatment necessary *and* perform the treatment. This authorization is granted only if I cannot be reached and a reasonable effort has been made to do so.

Date _____   Parent or guardian _____

Address _____   Phone ( )_____

Family physician _____   Phone ( )_____

Pre-existing medical conditions (e.g., allergies or chronic illnesses) _____

_____

Other(s) to also contact in case of emergency _____

Relationship to child _____   Phone ( )_____

My child and I are aware that participating in _____ is a potentially hazardous activity. I assume all risks associated with participation in this sport, including but not limited to falls, contact with other participants, the effects of the weather, traffic, and other reasonable risk conditions associated with the sport. All such risks to my child are known and understood by me.

I understand this informed consent form and agree to its conditions on behalf of my child.

Child's signature _____   Date _____

Parent's signature _____   Date _____

Equipment and Facilities Inspection

Another means of preventing injuries is to check the quality and suitability of all the equipment used by your wrestlers (e.g., headgear). Young wrestlers should wear headgear for practice and competition. Pay particular attention to the wrestling shoes; they must not have metal eyelets or rigid tips on the shoelaces. Wrestlers should remove rings, watches, and any other jewelry. Fingernails should be cut short, and a wrestler should not be allowed to practice or to compete if he has a skin infection or any kind of contagious disease.

Examine the mat and the area around it. The mat should be mopped with a disinfectant solution daily and immediately after it is bloodied by an injured nose, cut, or scrape. Remember that the out-of-bounds line is not a "fence." Move chairs, tables, clipboards, and any sharp or unyielding object that may be close to the mat. See that nearby walls and other immovable objects are padded. Report any conditions that you cannot remedy.

Before each day's practice, take a "safety walkaround" to look for potential problems. Has someone left a chair or table too near the mats? Has mat tape pulled loose, leaving a gap to step in? Has a condition you've already reported been corrected yet?

Matching Athletes by Maturity and Warning of Inherent Risks

Children of the same age can differ in height and weight by up to 6 inches and 50 pounds. Of course, in wrestling, contestants are paired by weight. But maturity and experience are also major factors in this combat sport. Matching a "novice" against a "veteran" with much greater experience and ability can expose the inexperienced athlete to serious injury. In practice and competition, try to arrange "novice" and "B team" events for your beginners, and don't allow your best wrestlers to enter such tournaments.

Matching athletes can help protect you from certain liability concerns. But you also must warn wrestlers and their parents of the risks involved in wrestling because "failure to warn" is one of the most successful arguments in lawsuits against coaches. Thoroughly explain the inherent risks of wrestling, and make sure each wrestler and his parents understand and appreciate those risks.

The preseason parent orientation meeting is a good opportunity to explain the risks of the sport to parents and prospective athletes. It is also a good occasion on which to have both the wrestlers and their parents sign waivers releasing you from liability should an injury occur. Such waivers do not relieve you of responsibility, but they are evidence that you have called attention to the risks of participation.

You may also want to demonstrate illegal and potentially dangerous holds and sitations to your wrestlers. Explaining the inherent danger of these moves and discouraging your wrestlers from executing them will protect both your athletes and yourself.

Proper Supervision and Record Keeping

With youngsters, your mere presence is not enough; you must actively plan and direct team activities and closely observe and evaluate wrestlers' participation. You're the watchdog responsible for their well-being. If you notice a player limping or grimacing, give him a rest and examine the extent of the injury.

As a coach, you're required to enforce the rules of the sport, prohibit dangerous horseplay, and hold practices only under safe conditions. These specific surpervisory activities will make the environment safer for your athletes and will help protect you from liability when mishaps occur.

For further protection, maintain a file of past season and practice plans, and keep records of your wrestlers' injuries. Season and practice plans come in handy when you need evidence that wrestlers have been taught certain skills; furthermore, accurate, detailed accident report forms offer protection against unfounded lawsuits. Ask for these forms from the organization to which you belong. And hold on to these records for several years so that an "old wrestling injury" of a former athlete doesn't come back to haunt you.

When it comes to injury prevention, you're the first one in and the last one out, and you're never "off duty." Horseplay is your worst enemy. Many of the really serious injuries in wrestling have come when kids were just "fooling around" during a momentary lapse in the coach's attention.

Warm-Up and Cool-Down

Although young bodies are generally very limber, they too can get tight from inactivity. Therefore, a warm-up period of approximately 10 minutes before each practice and match is strongly recommended. Warm-up should address each muscle group and get the heart rate elevated in preparation for strenuous activity. Easy running followed by stretching exercises is a common sequence.

As a practice is winding down, slow wrestlers' heart rates with an easy jog. Then arrange for a period of easy stretching at the end of practice to help the wrestlers avoid stiff muscles and make them less tight before the next session.

What If One of My Wrestlers Gets Hurt?

No matter how good and thorough your prevention program, injuries will occur.

When injury does strike, chances are you will be the one in charge. The severity and nature of the injury will determine how actively involved you'll be in treating the injury. But regardless of how seriously a wrestler is hurt, it is your responsibility to know what steps to take. So let's look at how you can provide *basic* emergency care to your injured athletes.

Minor Injuries

Although no injury seems minor to the person experiencing it, most injuries are neither life-threatening nor severe enough to restrict participation. When such injuries occur, you can take an active role in their initial treatment.

Sprains and Strains

The physical demands of wrestling most often result in injury to the muscles or tendons (strains) or to the ligaments (sprains). When your wrestlers suffer minor strains or sprains, immediately apply the RICE method of injury care.

R—Rest the area to avoid further damage and foster healing.

I— Ice the area to reduce swelling and pain.

C—Compress the area by securing an ice bag in place with a plastic wrap.

E—Elevate the injury above heart level to keep the blood from pooling in the area.

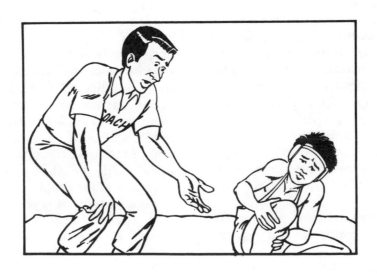

Bumps and Bruises

Inevitably, wrestlers make contact with each other and with the mat. If the force of a body part at impact is great enough, a bump or bruise will result. Most wrestlers continue participating with such sore spots, but if the bump or bruise is large and painful, you should react appropriately. Enact the RICE formula of injury care and monitor the injury. If swelling, discoloration, and pain have lessened, and the wrestler has complete function of the injured body part, he may resume participation with protective padding; if not, the wrestler should be examined by a physician.

Scrapes and Cuts

When one of your wrestlers has an open wound, follow these three steps:

1. Stop the bleeding by applying direct pressure with a clean dressing to the wound. *Do not* remove the dressing if it becomes blood-soaked. Instead, place an additional dressing on top of the one already in place. If the bleeding continues, elevate the injured area above the heart and maintain pressure.

2. Cleanse the wound thoroughly once the bleeding is controlled. A good rinsing with a forceful stream of water, and perhaps light scrubbing with soap, will help prevent infection.

3. Protect the wound with sterile gauze or a bandage. If the wrestler continues to participate, apply protective padding over the injured area.

For bloody noses not associated with a facial injury, have the athlete sit and lean slightly forward. Then pinch the wrestler's nostrils shut. If the bleeding continues after several minutes or if the athlete has a history of nosebleeds, seek medical assistance.

To protect yourself and others during treatment and cleanup of bleeding, wear disposable plastic gloves, use disposable towels, and keep a plastic bottle of diluted chlorine bleach solution handy. Mop up any blood that may be on the mat before resuming action.

Serious Injuries

Head, neck, and back injuries; fractures; and injuries that cause a wrestler to lose consciousness are among a class of injuries that you cannot and *should not try to treat yourself.* But you *should* plan what you'll do if such an injury occurs. And your plan should include the following guidelines for action:

- Obtain the phone number and ensure the availability of nearby emergency care units. Tape the phone numbers inside the lid of your first aid kit.
- Assign an assistant coach or another *adult* the responsibility of knowing the location of the nearest phone and calling emergency medical help upon your request.
- *Do not move* the injured athlete.
- Calm the injured athlete and keep others away from him as much as possible.
- Evaluate whether the athlete's breathing is stopped or irregular and, if necessary, clear the airway with your fingers.
- Administer artificial respiration if breathing has stopped. Administer cardiopulmonary resuscitation (CPR) or have an individual trained in CPR administer it if the athlete's circulation has stopped.
- Remain with the athlete until medical personnel arrive. If the injured wrestler must be taken to a hospital and if his parents are not available, have an adult that he knows accompany him.

How Do I Protect Myself?

When one of your wrestlers is injured, naturally your first concern is for his well-being. Your feelings for kids, after all, are what made you decide to coach. Unfortunately, there is something else that you must consider: Can you be held liable for the injury?

From a legal standpoint, a coach has nine duties to fulfill.

1. Provide a safe environment.
2. Properly plan each activity.

3. Provide adequate and proper equipment.

4. Match athletes by size, maturity, and skill.

5. Warn of inherent risks in the sport.

6. Supervise the activity closely.

7. Evaluate athletes for injury or incapacity.

8. Know emergency procedures and first aid.

9. Keep adequate records.

In addition to fulfilling these nine legal duties, you should check your organization's insurance coverage and your own to make sure the present policies protect you from liability.

Summary Self-Test

Now that you've read how to make your coaching experience safe for your wrestlers and yourself, test your knowledge of the material by answering these questions:

1. What are seven injury prevention measures you can institute to try to keep your wrestlers from being hurt?

2. What method of treatment is best for minor strains and sprains?

3. What is the three-step emergency care process for cuts?

4. What steps can you take to manage serious injuries?

5. What are the nine legal duties of a coach?

UNIT
6

What Is Wrestling All About?

From reading the first part of this manual, you now have a good general understanding of what it takes to be a coach. Now it's time to develop your comprehension of wrestling. This part of the book provides wrestling-specific information you will need to teach your athletes the sport.

Wrestling is the oldest form of recreational combat, arguably the oldest sport, with roots traced back thousands of years. Archaeologists have discovered ancient carvings and drawings in Africa, Europe, and Asia show-

ing wrestlers in holds and positions of leverage. Many of these holds and maneuvers are the same as those you will be teaching your kids.

How Do Kids Benefit From Wrestling?

Wrestling is a popular sport for kids. One particularly attractive feature is that wrestlers are matched up according to weight and age. This allows youngsters too small to compete in other sports to face opponents of approximately the same size and to compete in age-group programs from the preteens through adulthood. The benefits youngsters derive from wrestling are

- *physical development,*
- *nutritional awareness, and*
- *psychosocial growth.*

Physical Development

Good wrestlers at any level are in top physical condition. Any youngster who participates on a club or school team for a reasonable length of time stands to benefit physically and show greater

- flexibility,
- coordination,
- endurance,
- body awareness, and
- strength.

Admittedly, youngsters can get many of these benefits by participating in other sports. But in many sports, kids spend their time learning and trying to master skills used in that sport alone, such as hitting a baseball or dribbling a basketball. In contrast, wrestling promotes the learning of many general movement skills that can help youngsters succeed not only in wrestling but also in other activities.

Nutritional Awareness

Because wrestlers are grouped by weight as well as by age, youngsters are likely to develop good nutritional habits at an early age (see Unit 7). As a group, young wrestlers generally will be much more aware of nutrition than others their age. And wrestling's emphasis on both general conditioning and proper nutrition usually helps youngsters achieve the weight and percentage of body fat that is healthiest for them. But it won't happen automatically, so you must be prepared to provide them the nutritional guidance they need.

Psychosocial Growth

When youngsters participate in organized wrestling programs, they stand to benefit psychologically and socially from the

- increased self-responsibility,
- sense of achievement,
- added self-confidence,
- new friends, and
- exposure to new experiences.

When a wrestler steps onto the mat to face an opponent, his ability to perform effectively depends on his mind as well as his body. That's because this is a sport of action and reaction, and there simply isn't enough time for a wrestler to wait for instructions from

his coach. And, because every opponent is slightly different, no two matches are ever alike. In short, wrestlers learn to think on their feet and gain confidence to move forward without counsel.

Youngsters can feel a real sense of accomplishment when they win. What's just as important, however, is that they learn to accept responsibility for their losses. And in that regard, wrestling helps kids mature. As a coach, you play a major role in enabling them to learn and benefit from their experiences.

Underachievers, through wrestling, might gain the added self-confidence they need to be more successful in other aspects of their lives. Loners may gain new friends and become more adept at handling different social experiences. Plus, every kid who wrestles can learn about setting reasonable goals and working to achieve them, and about teamwork and fair play.

Without question, young wrestlers will encounter a variety of new situations. In practices, at matches, or on the road for tournaments, youngsters will be soaking in first-time experiences at every turn. They'll also be meeting new acquaintances along the way. You can help expand their horizons and social network by exposing them to as many positive opportunities and individuals as possible.

What Are the Rules?

Wrestling is not a highly complex sport. But because of the physical contact and exertion inherent in it, you must fully inform your wrestlers of the rules that do exist and make sure that they abide by them. Knowledge of the rules is also necessary to teach maneuvers and strategy properly.

Matches

All wrestling matches begin with the two wrestlers on their feet, facing each other in a neutral position, with no advantage to either one. The duration of a match is specified according to the wrestling style and the age group involved. It can be cut short by a fall, technical fall, injury, forfeit (failure to appear), or by disqualification for miscon-

duct, stalling, or any other violation of the rules the referee believes warrants it. Although wrestling is a "combat" sport, any hold or maneuver applied with the intent to injure the opponent is prohibited by the rules. A referee, timekeeper, and scorekeeper are necessary to conduct an official match.

Wrestling has two principal forms of competition:

- **Dual meets** between two teams, matching a wrestler from each team in each of several weight classes, and
- **tournaments**, in which several teams or several wrestlers enter in each weight class; team competition may or may not be involved.

Classification Systems

The wrestlers are matched up by weight and by age or grade in school. A weigh-in is held before the competition, and the wrestlers' body weight must be within certain limits specified for their age group and style of competition. The "unlimited" weight class no longer exists, so even the heaviest wrestlers must stay within established limits.

Equipment

Soft shoes with flat soles are required. The shoes may not have metal eyelets, and the rigid tips of shoelaces must be cut off. The one-piece uniform is called a *singlet*, under which the wrestler must wear an athletic supporter or underbrief. Protective headgear is required in folkstyle competition and is encouraged for young athletes in Olympic-style competition.

Wrestling takes place on a mat about an inch-and-a-half thick and some 25 to 30 feet across. The wrestling area is almost always circular. Modern mats are made of a foam-core plastic that is easily cleaned and has great cushioning capacity.

Terminology

Young wrestlers need to learn the language of the sport. Fortunately, the basic terminology of wrestling is almost self-explanatory.

Scoring maneuvers:

Takedown—taking the opponent down to the mat from neutral position.

Escape—getting away from the opponent, gaining a neutral position.

Reversal—an exchange of control, when the wrestler underneath gains the top position.

Near fall—a maneuver that almost, but not quite, brings a fall.

Time advantage—in collegiate wrestling only, a credit for the net time one wrestler spends in control of the other. Also called *riding time*.

Result of the match:

Fall—the ultimate objective, when one wrestler pins his opponent's shoulders to the mat for a specified time, ending the match.

Decision—a victory determined by points scored for takedowns, escapes, reversals, near falls, and, in some instances, time advantage.

Major decision—a decision by a specified margin of points in folkstyle.

Superior decision—a decision by a specified margin of points in freestyle.

Technical fall—a match that ends when a certain point spread is reached.

Draw—a match that ends with the score tied. If a tournament match ends in a draw, it is settled by an overtime period.

Default—the outcome of a match when one wrestler is injured and unable to wrestle or to continue wrestling.

Disqualification—a match in which a wrestler is declared the loser because he has violated the rules.

Forfeit—the outcome of a match in which one wrestler fails to appear.

What Are the Styles of Wrestling?

Many different wrestling styles are found around the world, including schwingen in Switzerland, glima in Iceland, sumo in Japan, and tchidaoba, kokh, gulech, and kurach in various republics of the Soviet Union. Each style has different rules, but all have virtually the same objective: to take the opponent from his feet to the ground, to turn him over (or to throw him on his back), and to hold his shoulders down.

Three types of wrestling are recognized and practiced in the United States, and, as a club or school coach, you probably will be involved in all three. High school and college wrestlers engage in *folkstyle* competitions, which emphasize taking an opponent down and controlling him on the mat.

Freestyle and *Greco-Roman* are the two international styles used in the modern Olympic Games. Freestyle is similar to folkstyle although it places less emphasis on control and more on turning the opponent's back toward the mat. The Greco-Roman style, which originated in Europe during the Napoleonic era, prohibits grasping the opponent's legs or using the legs to trip or hold the opponent. Because the legs can't be used to attack or defend, Greco-Roman often produces spectacular lifts and throws.

Folkstyle

These are the basic rules of scholastic wrestling. Collegiate rules vary somewhat, primarily in the number and limits on weight classes, the length of matches, and whether or not a minute of time advantage is worth a point.

Weight Classes

The high school level has 13 folkstyle weight classifications (in pounds):

up to 103	up to 145
up to 112	up to 152
up to 119	up to 160
up to 125	up to 171
up to 130	up to 189
up to 135	up to 275
up to 140	

The youth (pre-high school) level offers lower weight classes to accommodate very small wrestlers. For example, the 13 to 14 age group has a lower limit of 70 pounds; 11- to 12-year-olds start as low as 60 pounds; and kids 9 to 10 can weigh as little as 50 pounds.

Although weight classes differ by age, the system for entering athletes into competitions is the same for all levels. In a dual meet, each team may enter one wrestler in each weight class. The same is true for most tournaments. However, in open tournaments, a school or club may enter as many wrestlers as it wishes, and individuals can enter on their own.

Match Structure

The match is divided into three periods. The first period starts with both wrestlers standing. The second and third periods can start with either (a) both wrestlers down on the mat, one in a position of advantage, or (b) with the wrestlers on their feet, in a neutral position. A coin toss determines which

wrestler gets his choice of position. The first period in a college match is 3 minutes and the second and third periods are 2 minutes each. High school matches follow the same format, but have 2-minute periods. Pre-high school matches have 1-minute periods or are shorter still.

Scoring

Depending upon the starting position for each period, the wrestlers try to score takedowns, escapes, reversals, and near falls, to control their opponents on the mat, to turn them over, and then to pin their shoulders for a fall. Successful execution of these maneuvers is rewarded with match points.

Here's how the various maneuvers and penalties are scored:

• Takedown	2 points
• Escape	1 point
• Reversal	2 points
• Near fall	2 or 3 points (depending on the length of time a wrestler is held on his back)
• Time advantage	1 point for net time of a minute or more. High school and youth wrestling do not award a point for this.

A fall is called when an opponent's shoulders are pinned to the mat and held for 2 seconds (high school and college). If neither wrestler scores a fall, the winner is determined by the number of points earned. A victory by 8 or more points is a major deci-

sion. A margin of 15 points is a technical fall and ends the match.

In a dual meet, the performance of each wrestler determines whether his team receives points and how many. A decision is worth 3 points; a major decision, 4; a technical fall, 5; and a fall, 6. The loser receives no points, while a draw scores 2 points for each team. Winning by injury default, forfeit, or disqualification counts the same as a fall.

Tournaments

In a tournament, the brackets on which wrestlers' names appear determine the order of pairing. Winners advance to face other winners until one becomes champion. Top-rated wrestlers are oftentimes placed in opposite brackets, a practice called *seeding*, so that they will not be paired against each other until the final matches. Almost all tournaments have a consolation or double-elimination format, so that a wrestler who has lost only once still has an opportunity to place in the standings.

It is customary to award the successful wrestlers some token of achievement, traditionally medals or ribbons for first, second, and third places. In large tournaments, additional places are often recognized. In team competition, teams receive points for the placings of their individuals and bonus points when their wrestlers win by falls, technical falls, or major decisions. Winning teams receive trophies.

Freestyle

Whereas folkstyle is officiated by one referee, freestyle matches require three officials, two of whom must agree on any ruling. This international style is much faster and more spectacular than folkstyle.

Weight Classes

Freestyle wrestling also has 10 weight classes for adult competition. The lightest weight category is up to 105.5 pounds, whereas the upper limit on the heaviest class is 286 pounds.

As in folkstyle, youth competition offers more weight classes to choose from, and the limits are scaled to allow very small wrestlers to compete against others their size.

Match Structure

A match is one continuous period of 5 (adult and high school), 4 (ages 11 to 14), or 3 (10 and under) minutes. Wrestlers start the competition on their feet.

This international style requires wrestlers to be aggressive and to be willing to take risks in order to score. Officials are quick to penalize wrestlers for stalling, intentionally going out of bounds, or otherwise limiting the action.

Scoring

The scoring system used in freestyle is not quite as clear-cut as that used in folkstyle. Points are awarded for the spectacular nature of some maneuvers and not just for the maneuver itself. The greater the risk and the more advanced the technique, the more points it earns. Points tend to be scored much more quickly in freestyle than in folkstyle.

Here is a breakdown of the scoring used in this wrestling style:

- Takedown   1 to 5 points

Taking the opponent to the mat under control is 1 point. Taking him from his feet and then to his back scores 2 points. Taking him from his feet directly to his back scores 3 points. But if a wrestler takes the opponent from his feet to his back with a spectacular, high-arching throw, he receives 5 points.

- Escape   0 points

Technically, there is no such thing as an escape in freestyle wrestling. If the wrestlers are down on the mat with no particular action in progress, the officials stand them up and start them again in a neutral position.

- Reversal   1 point

A reversal in freestyle is the same as in folkstyle. It is an exchange of control, when the wrestler underneath gains the top position.

- Exposure   2 points

Exposure is freestyle's equivalent of the near fall and is defined as turning the opponent's back past a 90-degree vertical line with the mat, his head, shoulder, or elbow touching the mat. The exposure can be instantaneous, and there is no counting of time. If the exposure is the result of a lift and throw, it can be awarded 3 or 5 points. A fall is called in about half a second.

Kids' wrestling has its own modifications of the international rules. Certain maneuvers with a high risk of injury, such as the most spectacular lifts and throws, are prohibited in youth competition. And a fall must be controlled and held for two seconds, so that an inexperienced youngster is less likely to "pin himself" by mistakenly rolling across his own shoulders.

Freestyle dual meets are held between clubs, schools, and even countries. Team points are awarded differently, too:

- Fall   4 points

A technical fall (15-point margin) or an injury default, forfeit, or disqualification is considered equal to a fall and also scores 4 points.

- Superior decision   3.5 points for a victory by a margin of 12 to 14 points.
- Decision   3 points for a victory by a margin of 11 points or less.

If a losing wrestler scores at least one point during his bout, his team is awarded either 1 point (decision) or half a point (superior decision). A wrestler who loses by a fall or by a shutout does not earn any points for his team. A draw is not allowed. If a match ends in a tie, the wrestlers go directly into sudden-death overtime, first point winning the match.

Tournaments

Freestyle tournaments place the wrestlers' names on a chart by the drawing of numbers, rather than seeding. The contestants are divided into two groups, or pools. Preliminary rounds take place until all but three wrestlers in each pool have been eliminated by a second defeat. Those three compete against each other to determine placing within their group.

The winners of the two groups compete in the finals for first and second places. The runners-up in the groups wrestle for third and fourth places, and so on. Team awards are also presented.

Greco-Roman

Greco-Roman rules are the same as those for freestyle, with two exceptions. A Greco-Roman wrestler is not allowed to attack his opponent's legs, nor is he permitted to use his own legs to trip, lift, or execute other holds (including defensive holds). Refer to the freestyle section for weight classes, match structure, scoring, and the tournament system used in Greco-Roman.

What Style Do I Teach?

As a youth coach you will concentrate on teaching the basic skills, but the style of wrestling your athletes compete in will dictate some of the techniques, holds, and maneuvers you teach.

In both folkstyle and freestyle, the most important techniques are those that take the opponent to the mat. Single-leg and double-leg takedowns, the fireman's carry, arm drag, duck-under, heel pick, and inside trip are maneuvers to get the opponent off his feet and down to the mat. Of course, opposing coaches will be teaching the same things, so your wrestlers will need to learn defenses and counters against these techniques.

Sometimes the opponents will gain an advantage or score first, so your folkstyle wrestlers will have to know how to escape or score a reversal. The more common folkstyle techniques of sitout, standup, shoulder roll, and switch are seldom used in freestyle because they put the wrestler at risk of exposure without the potential reward of an escape point. However, there have been Olympic champions who relied on their past folkstyle experience to reverse for a victory.

Standard techniques for turning the opponent over, such as the half nelson, arm bar, and cradle, are fundamental moves in both folkstyle and freestyle. Eventually your wrestlers should learn a couple of "big" moves (e.g., a throw) to attempt when they need a bunch of points in a hurry at the end of a losing match.

Don't bother with exposure moves such as the crotch lift and gut wrench during the folkstyle season because wrestlers usually can't score with these moves under folkstyle rules. And when your team is learning Greco-Roman, don't spend time on single-leg and double-leg takedowns, trips, or other techniques that are prohibited by the rules. Instead, teach duck-unders, arm throws, lifts, and rolls through a bridge (gut wrench).

Every technique or maneuver you teach should include the stages of setup, execution, and follow-through. And don't forget the methods of defense and counterattack that have been developed specifically for each offensive move.

Expose Wrestlers to All Styles

The transition from folkstyle to the international styles won't be difficult for a fundamentally sound wrestler. In fact, American wrestlers who go on to compete in world events are noted for being particularly well-conditioned, well-disciplined athletes. This conditioning and discipline result partially from the demands of folkstyle, in which a wrestler must learn how to dominate, control, and wear down his opponent.

Folkstyle wrestlers can also benefit from international style competition. The daring approach required in freestyle and Greco-Roman challenges wrestlers to add new dimensions to their technical skills.

Summary Test

Now that you've read the basic wrestling information in this unit, you should be able to answer a number of questions about the sport. To test yourself, match up each of the following terms with the correct definition by placing the letter associated with the term on the answer blank next to the appropriate numbered item:

a. Dual meet   f. Near fall
b. Exposure   g. Reversal
c. Folkstyle   h. Takedown
d. Freestyle   i. Tournament
e. Greco-Roman   j. Weight class

1. ____ A style of wrestling practiced in American scholastic programs, placing emphasis on control of the opponent.

2. ____ Upper and lower limits on the weight of each wrestler so they can be matched according to size.

3. ____ Competition between two teams, consisting of a series of matches between wrestlers of approximately the same weight.

4. ____ A modern international style of wrestling where the wrestler may not attack his opponent's legs nor use his own legs to hold or lift.

5. _____ A scoring maneuver in which a wrestler takes his opponent to the mat under control.

6. _____ A nearly successful attempt to pin the opponent that scores points.

7. _____ Turning the opponent's back toward the mat past a 90-degree vertical line.

8. _____ A modern international style of wrestling that closely resembles the techniques practiced in folkstyle.

9. _____ An exchange of control in which the wrestler who is underneath gains an advantage over his opponent.

10. _____ Competition among a large number of wrestlers, grouped by weight classes, who often represent the many teams entered.

Answers: 1-c, 2-j, 3-a, 4-e, 5-h, 6-f, 7-b, 8-d, 9-g, 10-i.

UNIT 7

How Do I Get My Athletes in Shape?

The good news is that wrestling encourages top physical conditioning. The bad news is that some wrestling coaches encourage harmful weight loss that is dangerous to a young athlete's health. The best news is that the bad news doesn't have to happen.

Because of its weight classification system and the amount of physical contact, no other sport creates as much weight awareness among athletes as wrestling. Unfortunately, too much weight sensitivity may result in

unhealthy dietary behavior. This unit will describe how you can help your wrestlers manage their weight effectively.

Nutrition, physical conditioning, and weight control are part of an athlete's total fitness package. However, you do not need to be a nutritionist, exercise physiologist, or dietician to provide your athletes the basic information and activities they need to get, and stay, in shape. Simply read this unit and a few of the many fitness and health books available through ACEP and USA Wrestling, and you'll be prepared to advise and direct your wrestlers responsibly.

What Fitness Components Should Wrestlers Develop?

No athlete, particularly a wrestler, can afford to develop one part of his body or one component of his physical fitness at the expense of another. Adequate strength and endurance and good speed, balance, and range of motion are characteristics of the most successful wrestlers. So, to attain maximum potential, wrestlers must develop these fitness components:

- Flexibility
- Endurance
- Strength
- Speed
- Balance

Flexibility

Adequate range of motion at all body joints is a must for wrestling participation. Muscles that are tight and restrict movement not only limit performance, they also represent an injury waiting to happen!

So, from the very first practice session to the very last meet, emphasize the importance of proper warm-up to your wrestlers. Each muscle group should be stimulated and lengthened. Stretches should be to the point of slight discomfort, then held in that position for several counts. Each muscle group should be stretched at least three times, with a period of relaxation between stretches. If a wrestler's particular muscle group fails to loosen up after initial stretching, he should use it in a brief period of light activity, then attempt to stretch it out again.

The cool-down also is essential for flexibility. After practices and matches, have your wrestlers take at least 5 minutes to stretch the muscles they used. They'll be less tight before the next workout and experience less muscle soreness.

Endurance

As much as a wrestler needs to have heart on the mat to win, he also needs to condition his heart long before the match begins. A strong, well-conditioned cardiovascular system (heart and blood vessels) will enable his body to receive more oxygen and a higher volume of blood with every pump of the heart. And it will allow the wrestler to sustain a high level of exertion for a long time. Obviously, such cardiovascular conditioning will enhance both the youngster's health and his wrestling performance.

An excellent way to strengthen the cardiovascular system is to put it under controlled stress through progressively intense aerobic exercise, which promotes the intake of oxygen. Most individuals prefer running, but cycling, calisthenics, circuit weight training, and aerobic dance are effective alternatives.

Cardiovascular benefits from such activities are produced when the athlete's heart rate remains at about 70 percent of its maximum for at least 25 minutes. To calculate the optimum heart rate, subtract the athlete's age in years from 220, then multiply by 70 percent. Thus, a 12-year-old who sustains a heart rate of 145 beats per minute for half an hour would benefit aerobically from the workout. The heart rate "target zone" is 65 to 80 percent of maximum. Wrestlers must engage in such exercise sessions at least three times a week to experience cardiovascular benefits.

Strength

The development of muscular strength through resistance training is an important

part of total body conditioning. But any such programs should be prepared by a qualified athletic trainer, tailored for the age group involved. Because lifting is one of the Seven Basic Skills, we will discuss the fundamentals of lifting in Unit 8. Young wrestlers may get all the lifting they need during everyday practice. However, some may benefit from strengthening specific muscle groups.

The best conditioning tool, along with running, is wrestling practice and the vigorous physical activity involved in drills, repetitions, and competition. If you structure your practices correctly, your wrestlers should get much of the resistance work they need through the lifting they do in drills and conditioning exercises.

Speed and Balance

Some coaches attribute fitness and performance components to gifts of nature. They believe in the term "natural athlete." And speed and balance are two abilities on their "either he's got it or he doesn't" list.

So what do you do if your roster includes several slow-moving, stumbling wrestlers? Don't give up just yet! Many informed coaches and countless athletes can attest to the fact that speed and balance can be improved through proper training. Ballistics—quick, explosive movements— are especially effective for wrestlers. So have your athletes routinely engage in drills that require them to move in short bursts. Because body position and footwork are keys to balance, include a variety of agility drills in your workouts. You and your wrestlers will be surprised at the results.

When Is Good Nutrition Important?

Just as a car runs best with a full tank of the proper fuel, an athlete's body will perform at its maximum only when it's filled with the right "nutritional fuel." For active athletes, that fuel consists of complex carbohydrates. During digestion, carbohydrate is broken down into glucose, an important energy source used by muscles during exercise.

A healthy, growing kid needs a balanced diet, including three meals a day in moderate portions. His diet should include foods from the four major food groups: dairy, meat, fruit and vegetable, and grain. The youngster should avoid high-fat, high-sugar foods and snacks such as potato chips, soft drinks, mayonnaise, candy bars, and ice cream. His diet should emphasize foods that are rich in complex carohydrates, such as cereals, pasta, baked potatoes, and vegetables.

If you think nutrition starts and stops the week of the match, you're mistaken. Nutrition and hydration play important—and different—roles throughout the season. For our purposes, however, the following nutrition needs are greatest

- throughout training and practice,
- before and during competition, and
- following competition.

Training and Practice

Throughout the season the young wrestler needs a regular diet that supplies energy to support his training and practice schedule. A well-balanced diet rich in complex carbohydrates is essential for supplying energy and building muscle glycogen levels. How many calories a wrestler needs depends on how many calories he burns each day. This isn't always easy to determine because the energy burned varies with body size, body composition, and the intensity and duration of workouts. You should consult an athletic trainer or a sports medicine physician to design a diet matched to the wrestler's specific caloric requirements.

The Pre-Event Meal

Many wrestlers don't understand the exact role of the pre-event meal. It has little effect on endurance because it takes 2 or 3 days for foods to increase muscle glycogen levels. However, the pre-match meal is important for increasing blood glucose and liver glycogen stores, energy sources used in the early stages of competition. If blood glucose levels are high at the start of the match, the wrestler will be able to compete longer before having to use muscle glycogen stores.

To avoid stomach upset, nausea, or a "stuffed" feeling, tell your wrestlers to eat the meal 3 to 4 hours before the match.

Advise them to avoid spicy, fatty foods. These are difficult to digest and may cause distress during the match. Also, discourage the intake of high-fat, high-protein foods like steaks, hamburgers, french fries, chips, and mayonnaise.

Conversely, cereals, pasta, baked potatoes, and muffins are good carbohydrate sources that are easily digested. Vegetables and fruit juices are also good pre-event foods, as are some dairy products such as low-fat yogurt, ice milk, and low-fat milk.

Post-Event Recovery

Because a wrestling match is continuous, a wrestler doesn't have a chance to replace body fluids during the competition itself. But he's losing body fluids by sweating and should replace them by sipping water as soon as the bout is over in order to help his body start its recovery period.

Recovering from the match is just as important as preparing for it, particularly in a tournament situation where the wrestler has several matches in one day. Even with regular fluid breaks, he may lose large quantities of body water in the form of sweat. And his muscle glycogen levels may be low, leaving him feeling weak and exhausted.

Now is the time to start the recovery process so he can resume practice and com-

petition with renewed energy and endurance. So encourage the wrestler to continue rehydrating for several hours after the event and to eat foods rich in carbohydrates to speed the rate of glycogen recovery.

What About Making Weight?

Wrestling is a sport for individuals of all shapes and sizes. This is one of our sport's greatest assets. However, the very weight-class system that allows both the big man and the little man to achieve success also lends itself to abuse by wrestlers, coaches, and parents. Specifically, weight cutting and manipulation of body fluids is harmful to both the health of the individual and the reputation of the sport.

In striving for maximum performance, wrestlers and their coaches often overlook two key areas—nutrition and hydration. To lose unwanted pounds, they starve and dehydrate themselves, or they "bulk up" by eating and drinking large quantities to gain weight. Both dietary practices reduce strength and endurance.

The sad part of the story is that such behavior often is condoned, even encouraged, by adults who have lost perspective. The coach may be looking at an empty weight class in his lineup and thinking, "Wouldn't it be great if we could cut Billy down 10 pounds and have a bigger, stronger wrestler in that weight?'' But it's like cramming a size 9 foot into a size 7 shoe. It may be bigger, but it's not necessarily stronger, and it's going to hurt!

Parents too can pressure their kids to ''succeed'' by cutting weight. This pressure is oftentimes a product of the parent's ego and is something you should address in an early-season meeting.

We know that a competitive athlete should be hungry to perform and to win, but a young wrestler who is constantly hungry for food is likely to be unhappy and less effective. His discontent may well spread to his studies and to his social life. Both his physical and emotional health could be in danger.

Choosing a Proper Weight Class

Weight classes increase at intervals of as little as 5, 6, or 7 pounds, depending on the wrestling style. Because of this, many wrestlers are tempted to cut weight and compete against smaller opponents. Discourage such weight cutting and help your athletes find the proper weight class. Your wrestlers' health, happiness, and success are at stake.

For example, a high school wrestler who weighs 150 pounds may be caught between two weight classes. He can either drop 5 pounds and compete at 145 or compete under the 152-pound ceiling—perhaps against larger opponents who have dropped their own weight from 160 or more. The inclination of most wrestlers (and their coaches) in such situations is to embark immediately on a weight-loss program. Such a decision may cost the wrestler on the mat and off. He might not be as effective at 145 as he was at 150. His coach might better have advised him to put on a few pounds of muscle than to take off needed weight.

Determining Optimal Body Weight

Before selecting a weight class, the wrestler and his coach should determine his optimal competitive weight. This optimal weight is neither his lowest possible weight nor the

weight at which he can best make the lineup. It should be the boy's healthiest weight—the one at which he can perform most effectively without slowing his normal growth.

An accurate way to gauge optimal body weight is by the percentage of fat tissue in the body. This should be measured during the preseason medical examination by use of skinfold calipers or hydrostatic (underwater) weighing. The physician then will recommend whether the body fat percentage should be reduced.

Obviously, the health and performance of a wrestler with 25% body fat would improve if his percentage were reduced. Body fat can be lowered by reducing caloric intake, by raising the level of activity, or by a combination of the two. But a young wrestler whose body fat is below 10% may be well advised to increase his caloric intake.

Any weight control program should start a couple of months before the official start of the wrestling season. If weight loss is appropriate, help your wrestler chart an 8-week program of increased activity and lowered caloric intake. Follow the standard dietary advice found in this unit. Keep reminding the athlete that a very fast weight reduction is not the answer. Although he

may lose 3 pounds in a 24-hour period by fasting, two-thirds of that stems from water loss and a depletion of vital energy supplies of glucose and glycogen. Therefore, 2 pounds a week is as fast as weight should be reduced.

Check That Excess Baggage

If there is excess baggage in your body, it is not water. When you eat too much, your body stores the excess in fat. When you drink too much, your body simply eliminates whatever it cannot use. For this reason, young wrestlers should make a point of drinking several glasses of water every day. Encourage them to drink water occasionally instead of snacking; this will help curb the hunger and reduce the number of empty calories they are taking in.

Too many wrestlers try to squeeze into lower weight classes by constantly eliminating or restricting water from their bodies before weigh-in. This is just about the worst thing a wrestler can do. Whether water is eliminated quickly in a sauna, with the aid of a diuretic, or by restricting the intake of water, asking the body to function with a subnormal level of fluid is dangerous. Even when as much as 5 hours is allowed for rehydration after weigh-in, the balance between fluids and electrolytes cannot be completely reestablished; therefore, the wrestler remains dehydrated.

Studies by the American College of Sports Medicine clearly show that dehydration causes a loss of electrolytes, the electrical conductors that play an important role in maintaining the body's chemical balance. An electrolyte imbalance can diminish strength and coordination, slow reaction time, and affect heart, kidney, and neurological functioning. Such changes can impede normal growth and development and threaten youngsters' health.

Cut Out the Weight Cutting

Weight that comes off during training, conditioning, and by switching to a healthy, balanced diet is probably excess poundage that was detrimental to the athlete's health and wrestling performance. However, in youth wrestling any other weight should be maintained by wrestlers. At the high school level, there are regulations against dangerous weight-cutting practices. And on the college scene, success is more a matter of weight *control* and weight *management* than weight *cutting*. The National Collegiate Athletic Association, for example, has taken a strong stand against radical dehydration and its inherent health hazards.

The focus of weight reduction must be on physical fitness. Exercise is important in expending calories and also in maintaining a proper diet. Therefore, encourage the wrestler to continue workouts during his weight-reduction period. If the athlete must snack between meals, encourage him to choose fruit or vegetables rather than cookies or candy.

Finally, instruct and motivate the athlete to follow good nutritional practices every day, not just the day before a match. Praise and reward him for sticking to the program. And make clear to him that if he takes shortcuts on his diet or any part of his conditioning program, he can expect to suffer the consequences on the mat.

UNIT 8

What Wrestling Skills Should I Teach?

In Unit 4 you learned how to teach wrestling skills and techniques and to plan practices. Now it's time to consider exactly *what* skills to emphasize and what activities you'll use to help your wrestlers develop those techniques. This unit describes the Seven Basic Skills, suggests how to use them as a base for teaching specific maneuvers, and recommends a variety of drills you can use to develop your wrestlers' abilities.

This unit will not bombard you with technical descriptions of hundreds of maneuvers, variations, and counters. Nor will it chart separate courses according to age groups and styles of wrestling. Instead, it is based on the premise that, while rules change from one wrestling style to another, the basic skills required to perform *all* wrestling maneuvers do not change.

What Are the Seven Basic Skills?

Mastery of the basic wrestling skills is essential to the proper execution of all holds and maneuvers. The skills are the building blocks upon which all other instruction must be laid. The Seven Basic Skills lead to the development of specific techniques and maneuvers, in turn setting the stage for competition and strategy.

Good wrestlers have instinctively practiced sound fundamental skills for centuries. But don't leave your wrestlers' learning to chance. Teach them the Seven Basic Skills in a systematic manner.

- Skill 1—Position
- Skill 2—Motion
- Skill 3—Changing levels
- Skill 4—Penetration
- Skill 5—Lifting
- Skill 6—Back step
- Skill 7—Back arch

Skill #1: Position

Call it stance, call it posture, if you wish. By any term, proper body position—the ability of a wrestler to control specific parts of his body in relation to each other—is the first requirement for successful execution of any primary maneuver.

Your wrestler should assume a semisquatting position with his knees slightly bent and his feet approximately shoulder-width apart. This foot spread provides both a wide base of support for stability and good balance for quick motion. Instruct each wrestler to face his opponent directly, with the toes of both feet forming a plane with the chest. The other option is to have him face the opponent on an angle, with one foot in front of the other.

The key parts of the body and their proper relationship to each other are these:

- Knees—bent (flexed), never any farther in front of the body than the chest.
- Chest—up and out, always over a vertical plane with the knee.
- Hips—low, flexed, and over the supporting points on the mat.
- Feet—shoulder-width apart and under the center of gravity.
- Head—always up and above the shoulders.
- Hands—held in front of the hips, palms down.
- Elbows—flexed, held in close to the hips.
- Back—straight.

Wrestling has three fundamental positions: (a) neutral position, in which neither wrestler has an advantage; (b) top position, in which the wrestler is in control of his opponent; and (c) down position, in which the opponent is in control. Your wrestlers' actions and reactions from each of these positions are crucial to their success. Therefore, motion is the next Basic Skill you should teach.

Position Drills

T-Shirt Drill

To reinforce the critical need of keeping the elbows in close to the body, pull a T-shirt over the back of the wrestler's head. Leaving it attached to the arms, pull the T-shirt down his back until it pinches his elbows tightly to his sides. With correct posture, the T-shirt will strap the elbows in close to the body in the correct position for the arms. With enough practice, this position will become second nature to your wrestlers.

Wall Drill

Many wrestlers have trouble maintaining a stable back position, tending to bend at the waist and overextend the upper body. One of the simplest and most effective ways to teach them proper back position is the wall drill. Using the wall for support, have them bend their knees slightly, keeping their heads up. As they step away from the wall, they will be forced to lean forward just a little bit to keep their balance but should come as close as possible to their position against the wall. The straighter the wrestlers keep their backs, the more it becomes necessary to lower their hips by bending their knees. A lower center of gravity provides more stability.

Skill #2: Motion

Power is the result of two factors: strength and mobility. Regardless of how strong an individual may be, a wrestler's strength is of little value if he is unable to move the various parts of his body explosively into or away from his opponent. Maximum potential for quick movement, and thus maximum power, can be attained only through proper body position.

The ability to move laterally depends upon keeping the arms (hands) and legs (feet) free and the muscles flexed and ready to explode. An arm or a leg that has been straightened out or pinned to the wrestler's own body, to that of his opponent, or to the mat cannot be used until it has been brought back to a coiled position.

A wrestler must be able to move in a free and fluid manner, so coach your wrestlers to circle their opponents or move into or away from them. Smooth movement is the result of constant readjustment of the feet

with quick, short, choppy steps. A quick spin around a single point of support, (i.e., pivoting on one foot) enhances fast, smooth movement. Demonstrate the practical value of learning footwork skills by pointing out to your wrestlers that one of the important finishes to a single-leg takedown depends upon this type of smooth, pivoting motion. Once the opponent's leg has been secured, if he drives into your wrestler, a quick circular movement will split his base and set him down.

Motion Drill

Shadow Drill

Have your wrestlers square off with a partner, both assuming the proper body position and facing each other head-on. On the whistle, they start moving together laterally, shadowing each other's movements as closely as possible, and concentrating on short, quick, choppy steps. On a second whistle, they change direction, still shadowing each other. Watch that they do not extend the arms, move the elbows away from the hips, drop the head, or arch the back.

Individually, they should try a rapid series of circular movements, quartering first to the right, then to the left. These subtle changes in direction create new angles from which to attack the opponent. If you look carefully at a fireman's carry, you'll see how the initial forward motion is changed into a twisting rotation of the hips and legs, putting the wrestler in position to pull down on the arm and finish the carry.

Skill #3: Changing Levels

The skill that must precede the successful execution of any move is the ability to change levels in relation to the opponent and to the mat. This skill, unfortunately, is the one most often overlooked in the development of a good wrestler.

It represents nothing more than motion in a vertical plane. Although many wrestlers consider lowering or raising their heads as the equivalent of changing levels, it is the ability to raise and lower the *hips* while

remaining in good position that is the key to success of this vertical motion.

Teach your wrestlers that the only way to change levels is to bend at the knees—going to a low squat and keeping the head up. Only after properly changing levels and getting the hips down can a wrestler successfully move into his opponent. When executing a duck-under, an appropriate tug or snap on the opponent's head enables the wrestler to go down and immediately pop up behind him. Bending at the waist, however, leaves the wrestler vulnerable to a snapdown, arm drag, or front headlock.

Successful execution of a standup depends on proper change of levels. But once a wrestler gets to his feet, he should lower his hips (not bend his waist). He thus becomes heavier for the opponent, and it is easier to break his grip and turn to face him.

Changing Levels Drills

Back-to-Back Drill

Have each wrestler stand back-to-back with a partner—backs straight, elbows in tight to the body, arms out, heads up, and leaning back into each other so they support each other. On the whistle, the partners move laterally in unison, using short, choppy steps. On a second whistle, they lower their levels together into fuller squats while continuing to move together. Repeated several times, this drill coordinates lateral motion with the lowering of levels.

Limbo Stick Drill

Hold a limbo stick at chest height to your average wrestler. The wrestlers attempt to walk under it in a low squat with the hips leading the way, head up and back straight. The stick can be lowered as they gain control of this exercise.

Skill #4: Penetration

To move an opponent from a position of stability (a good stance) and to reduce his potential power (mobility), the wrestler eventually must make contact with and control his opponent's hips. To do so requires that any movement in his direction not be just *to* him, but literally *through* him!

This forward motion through him should be directed toward his hips or the location where his hips will be at a given instant. A line on the mat from the attacking wrestler to his opponent would run directly to his hips (through his legs) and to a point at least 3 feet beyond. We are talking about driving the hips *through* the opponent's hips.

When incorporated into a double-leg tackle, deep penetration will put the wrestler completely through his opponent before the opponent can react. It is important to remember that the step should not only be deep but also directed to the opponent's hips. The secret is not in stepping to where he was, but in anticipating where he's going to be.

Penetration Drill

Giant Stride Drill

This drill will help emphasize the concepts of sweeping through the opponent and lowering levels for stability. Using the distance from toe to knee as the interval, place 8 to 10 strips of tape across the floor or mat. Have the wrestler stand on the first strip and step forward with his right foot, lowering his level into a squatting position. The right foot should reach the second strip of tape.

The right thigh and calf should now form a 90-degree angle with each other. From this position, the hips are thrust forward so the right knee is driven to the third strip of tape. Now the left foot is swung into the lead position and onto the fourth strip. The wrestler continues striding in this manner until he reaches the last strip of tape. Then he spins around on the knee that is down and strides back to the starting point.

The tape strips help the wrestler gauge his stride and overcome the tendency to step too far forward. Of course, you'll have to put down several sets of strips for different-size wrestlers. In addition to being a good penetration drill, the giant stride is an excellent stretching and warm-up exercise.

Skill #5: Lifting

Of all the basic skills, the ability to lift is probably the most important. Too often, however, wrestlers believe that they do not have enough strength. And they probably won't if they use only the arms. You see, the strongest muscles in the body are located in the hips and thighs. Although strength is important, the ability to lift depends more upon the position of the hips to the opponent than anything else.

The key steps to teach your wrestlers to lift an opponent follow.

1. Squeeze your opponent to your body with your arms. Do not try to pull him up with the strength of your arms. Simply "secure" him. Regardless of what part of his body you secure, or your position to him (front, back, or side), the two following points apply.
2. Lower your hips into and under his center of gravity (his hips).
3. Lift up with the power in your legs and keep your hips driven into and under him (penetration).

One of the most exciting confrontations in a wrestling match is when two good wrestlers are struggling in an upright position. The wrestler behind tries to keep control of his opponent and get into a position to lift, while the wrestler in front struggles to break his opponent's grasp by lowering his level and extending his arms.

Another interesting matchup occurs when one man gets to the side of his opponent after executing a duck-under but finds himself momentarily stymied. From this position, he must get his hips down and into the opponent to finish the lift and score.

The lift is also an integral part of the high crotch takedown. The same principles apply. The arms are used to secure the opponent. The forward thrust of the hips and straightening of the back provide upward momentum, and the lift ensures a successful finish.

Lifting Drills

Up-in-Arms Drill

Have the wrestler lift a fairly heavy weight over his head by using only the strength of his arms. Note the degree of difficulty. Then execute the press again by using the fundamentals of Skill #5. The lift should be noticeably easier.

Body Lift Drill

The wrestlers should practice actual body lifts with a partner, each using the other as dead weight. Facing his partner, the wrestler wraps his arms around the other's torso, lowers his level, thrusts his hips forward to penetrate, and lifts with his legs. Then they may alternate belly-to-back lifts. The wrestlers should concentrate on using the arms as nothing more than hooks to secure the opponent, changing levels, and lifting with the legs.

Reverse Lift and Turn

This is a good conditioning exercise. One wrestler takes his opponent in a reverse waistlock position and lifts him to his own waist. He then rotates the opponent (head down) until the opponent's head is outside of his other leg. He then sets the opponent down. This can be repeated several times.

Skill #6: Back Step

The back step gets a wrestler into a specific position from which he can lift the opponent. This skill requires the ability to smoothly and quickly rotate the hips into and under the opponent, so that the opponent ends up behind him and over his hips.

The smooth, quick rotation can be accomplished by bringing the feet close together to create a small point of support, much like that of a child's toy top. From this position, the wrestler can change levels (Skill #3), rotate his hips "to and through" the opponent (Skill #4), and be in position to lift (Skill #5).

The back step can position a wrestler for a headlock and a variety of other maneuvers. Maneuvers involving the back step are dis-

tinguished by what part of the opponent's body is secured. If it is the head and arm that are tied up, it's a headlock; if the hold is over one arm and under the other, it's a hiplock.

Back Step Drills

Beginner's Back Step Drill

Have the wrestler face his partner, securing him behind the neck with the right hand and grasping his right elbow with the left hand. Now the backstep motion should be executed with the feet close together.

Rope Drill

To practice the movement without lifting, attach a rope to the wall or to a post at shoulder height. This can be used to provide balance and stability as the wrestler brings his feet close together and practices spinning. Without a partner or an aid, it is difficult to spin and maintain balance.

Skill #7: Back Arch

The back arch leads to another very specific positon from which to lift. The back arch requires the ability to balance one's own body over a point of support while driving the hips into and under the opponent (Skill #4) and going from the feet into a high-arching back bridge. In its ultimate form, it gives rise to the spectacular lifts and throws associated with the international styles. Although some of these throws are not legal under folkstyle and youth rules, the basic arch is found in many of the maneuvers used by top athletes.

The fireman's carry is a perfect example of a move that includes the back arch. The hips are kept in, and the arch is used to throw the opponent to his back. The back arch also is important on all throws, along with the head-outside single-leg, duck-unders, and every maneuver that requires a lift (Skill #5).

Back Arch Drill

Beginner's Back Arch Drill

The key to mastering this skill is to bend the knees while moving the hips forward and leaning backward into a bridge. Within a few weeks, the wrestler should be able to arch into a bridge and touch his forehead to the mat without using his arms. The bridge can come in handy as a last-ditch maneuver to avoid a pin.

It is important that your wrestlers practice the skill in steps and with the assistance of a partner. Check the extent to which each wrestler can control his own body when going back into the arch. When performed properly, little if any weight is distributed to the head. The continued thrust of the hips forward counterbalances the weight of the upper body arching backward. The result is that the center of gravity remains over the points of support, the feet.

The wrestler should start in a squat to get the feel of moving his hips forward while the upper body goes back. If the hips are moving forward, there will be little need for the partner's help. When the wrestler finds himself pulling on his partner's arm, it's a signal to drive the hips forward and redistribute his weight.

Putting It All Together

Just because you have taught all Seven Basic Skills effectively, that doesn't mean your wrestlers will always perform them successfully in matches. Their opponents will have more than a little to say about the results of their attempts to apply the skills. However, you need to encourage your wrestlers to develop analytical skills so that they can determine the skill at which they faltered.

For example, if one of your wrestlers attemps the basic single-leg attack and the opponent counters with pressure, your wrestler should know to return immediately to square one. First, he should make certain that he is carrying his body (position) correctly. Then he should move on to Skill #2, lateral, forward, or circular motion, and try to create a new and better angle of attack. Once a good angle is achieved, the wrestler should try changing levels (Skill #3) to gain an advantage. Hopefully, after the wrestler moves through each of the Seven Basic Skills, he will find the key to lifting and scoring on his opponent.

Learning the sequence of the Seven Basic Skills allows wrestlers to see that all of the many wrestling maneuvers have simple, standard components. This unit should help you teach your wrestlers these fundamentals. And if you do a good job of it, they'll enjoy the sport and probably experience success in their future wrestling matches.

This manual should serve as a stepping-stone for you to learn more about wrestling and about coaching. With a solid foundation gained through this book, you should be prepared to move on to teaching wrestlers how to set up, execute, and follow through with a single-leg, duck-under, or fireman's carry. And you should also be ready to learn more about communicating with athletes, teaching them sport skills, and providing them dietary guidance. USA Wrestling and the American Coaching Effectiveness Program have the courses and learning resources you need to develop your coaching potential.

Take the Next Step . . .

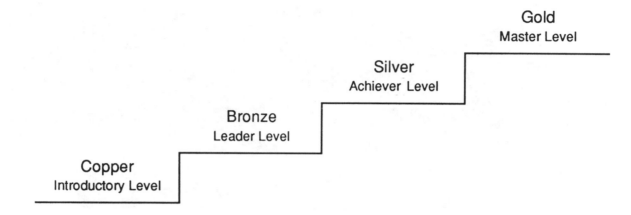

Gold
Master Level

Silver
Achiever Level

Bronze
Leader Level

Copper
Introductory Level

The National Coaches Education Program (NCEP) is part of the continuing efforts of USA Wrestling to broaden the base of knowledgeable, competent, and effective coaches in the sport of wrestling.

When you've completed the Copper Introductory Leader Level, you will be ready to move up to the Bronze Leader Level. The Bronze is designed to provide information to coaching leaders about training programs for developing wrestlers. Requirements for Bronze certification include attending the USA Wrestling Bronze Leader Level education clinics, 1 year of coaching experience, and successful completion of written exams covering the content of this level of the program.

After completing the Bronze Leader Level, you may advance to the Silver Achiever Level. This level of instruction is designed for coaches who are interested in developing a more concentrated and intense training program for experienced wrestlers. The basic disciplines introduced for Bronze certification will be studied in more detail and at greater depth. Requirements for Silver certification include 3 years of coaching experience and participation in a USA Wrestling Silver Achiever Level clinic held in conjunction with a USA Total Wrestling Camp.

The highest level of coaching recognized by USA Wrestling is the Gold Master Level. Instruction at this level is designed for the full-time, career-minded coach, dedicated to the development of wrestlers for national and international teams. Prospective Gold Master Level coaches should write to USA Wrestling for certification requirements.

National Coaches Education Program
developed by

USA Wrestling
225 South Academy
Colorado Springs, CO 80910

Appendix: Sample Season Plan for Wrestlers

Sample Season Plan for Wrestlers

Goal: To help youngsters learn the fundamental skills of the sport and to compete in local and state competitions.

T: Teach and practice the skill initially for a given duration (minutes).

D: Review the skill and drill for a given duration (minutes).

Skills/Drills	Week 1 Day 1	Week 1 Day 2	Week 2 Day 1	Week 2 Day 2	Week 3 Day 1	Week 3 Day 2	Week 4* Day 1	Week 4* Day 2	Week 5* Day 1	Week 5* Day 2	Week 6* Day 1	Week 6* Day 2	Week 7* Day 1	Week 7* Day 2	Week 8** Day 1	Week 8** Day 2
Warm-up	T(15)	D(10)	D(15)	D(10)	D(10)	D(10)	D(10)	D(10)	D(10)	D(10)	D(10)	D(10)	D(10)	D(10)	D(10)	D(10)
Seven Basic Skills	T(30)	T(15)	D(15)	D(10)	D(10)	D(5)	D(5)	D(5)	D(5)	D(5)	D(5)	D(5)	D(5)	D(5)	D(5)	D(3)
Tie-ups	T(15)	D(5)	D(10)	D(5)	D(5)	D(5)	D(3)	D(3)			D(5)	D(3)	D(5)	D(5)	D(3)	D(3)
Single leg	T(20)		D(10)	D(5)	D(5)		D(3)	D(3)	D(3)	D(3)	D(3)	D(3)	D(5)		D(3)	D(3)
Double leg		T(15)	D(10)	D(5)	D(5)		D(3)	D(3)	D(3)	D(3)	D(3)	D(3)	D(5)	D(3)	D(3)	D(3)
Whizzer					T(15)	D(5)				D(3)				D(3)		
Pancake							T(10)	D(3)	D(5)		D(10)	D(3)	D(5)		D(3)	D(3)
Headlock							T(10)	D(3)	D(5)		D(10)	D(3)	D(5)		D(3)	D(3)
Snapdown									T(10)	D(5)	D(5)	D(3)	D(3)		D(3)	D(3)
Butt drag									T(10)	D(5)	D(5)	D(3)	D(3)		D(3)	D(3)
Half nelson		T(15)	D(5)	D(5)		D(5)	D(5)	D(5)		D(5)						
Chicken wing				T(10)	D(5)	D(10)		D(5)			D(10)	D(10)				
Laced ankles						T(15)	D(5)	D(10)		D(10)	D(10)	D(10)	D(10)	D(10)		D(10)
Bridging	T(5)	D(5)	D(5)	D(5)	D(5)											
Par terre defense						T(10)	D(5)	D(5)		D(5)		D(5)				
Scrimmage	T(5)	D(10)	D(15)	D(15)	D(20)	D(15)	D(18)	D(17)	D(16)	D(26)	D(21)	D(21)	D(21)	D(17)	D(16)	D(16)
Conditioning				T(15)	D(10)	D(10)	D(10)	D(10)	D(10)	D(10)	D(10)	D(10)	D(10)	D(10)	D(10)	
Cool-down	T(10)	D(10)	D(5)	D(5)	D(5)	D(5)	D(5)	D(5)	D(5)	D(10)	D(10)	D(10)	D(10)	D(10)	D(10)	D(10)
Elapsed time	75	90	90	90	90	90	90	90	90	105	100	105	90	75	75	70

Note: A computer software spreadsheet program can be a helpful tool in designing training plans.

*Wrestlers will participate in a dual meet or local tournament on the third activity day of the week.

**Wrestlers will participate in a dual meet or state tournament on the third activity day of the week.

Wrestling and Coaching Books

Successful Coaching
(Second Edition)

Rainer Martens, PhD

1990 • Paper • 248 pp
Item PMAR0376
ISBN 0-88011-376-6
$16.00 ($20.00 Canadian)

Revised to meet the needs of secondary school coaches and others who have a beginning knowledge of coaching, this book is the most widely read coaching book ever written.

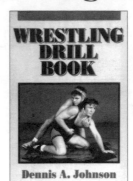

Wrestling Drill Book
Dennis A. Johnson, MS

1991 • Paper • 248 pp
Item PJOH0401
ISBN 0-88011-401-0
$17.00 ($21.50 Canadian)

Featuring 169 drills for teaching basic wrestling skills, this book emphasizes development of position, motion, level change, penetration, backstep, lifting, and back arch.

Successful Wrestling
Coaches' Guide for Teaching Basic to Advanced Skills

Art Keith, EdD

1990 • Paper • 160 pp
Item PKEI0329
ISBN 0-88011-329-4
$20.00 ($25.00 Canadian)

Organized by skill progressions rather than by types of skills, this coaching tool takes you step-by-step through 30 wrestling techniques, from simple to complex.

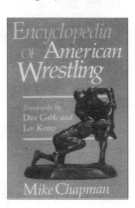

Encyclopedia of American Wrestling
Mike Chapman

Forewords by Dan Gable, World and Olympic Champion, and Lee Kemp, World and NCAA Champion

1990 • Paper • 544 pp
Item PCHA0342
ISBN 0-88011-342-1
$24.95 ($30.95 Canadian)

This is the most detailed chronicle ever written on the people and places that have made wrestling history.

Wrestling Fundamentals and Techniques

The Iowa Hawkeyes' Way

Mark Mysnyk, MD

1982 • Paper • 208 pp
Item PMYS0098
ISBN 0-918438-98-5
$16.95 ($20.95 Cndn)

An Illustrated Guide to Teaching Kids to Wrestle

Bill Martell

1985 • Paper • 160 pp
Item PMAR0000
ISBN 0-88011-000-7
$14.95 ($18.50 Cndn)

Nick and the Cyclones

Mike Chapman

1989 • Cloth • 152 pp
Item PCHA0291
ISBN 0-88011-291-3
$19.95 ($24.95 Cndn)

The New Breed

Living Iowa Wrestling

Lou Banach with Mike Chapman

1985 • Paper • 136 pp
Item PBAN0258
ISBN 0-88011-258-1
$14.00 ($17.50 Cndn)

They Call It Wrestling

A Pictorial Anthology of the American Wrestler

Wade Schalles

1983 • Cloth • 288 pp
Item PSCH0074
ISBN 0-88011-074-0
$35.00 ($43.50 Cndn)

ACEP Volunteer Level

The American Coaching Effectiveness Program (ACEP) now provides two excellent youth coaches' courses: the Rookie Coaches Course and Coaching Young Athletes Course. The Rookie Coaches Course not only introduces coaches to the basic principles of coaching, but also teaches them how to apply those fundamentals as they instruct young athletes in the rules, skills, and strategies of their particular sport. This *Rookie Coaches Wrestling Guide* serves as a text for the course.

The second coaching education option at the Volunteer Level is the Coaching Young Athletes Course. This alternative is for coaches who have completed the Rookie Coaches Course successfully and coaches who want to receive more instruction in the principles of coaching than is offered in that course.

ACEP encourages youth sport coaches to complete both the Rookie Coaches and Coaching Young Athletes Courses. We believe the combined learning experiences afforded by these courses will give you the coaching background you need to be the kind of coach kids learn from and enjoy playing for.